JOHNS ISLAND
PRESBYTERIAN CHURCH

JOHNS ISLAND
PRESBYTERIAN CHURCH

ITS PEOPLE AND ITS COMMUNITY
FROM COLONIAL BEGINNINGS
TO THE TWENTY-FIRST CENTURY

CHARLES E. RAYNAL, PhD

Charleston   London

THE
History
PRESS

Published by The History Press
Charleston, SC 29403
www.historypress.net

Copyright © 2010 by Charles E. Raynal
All rights reserved

Front Cover photo by Julie Foster
Back Cover photos by Katharine Bair. Image of the Archibald Stobo Bible used by
permission of the South Carolina Historical Society, Charleston.

First published 2010

Manufactured in the United States

ISBN 978.1.59629.950.4

Library of Congress Cataloging-in-Publication Data

Raynal, Charles Edward, 1943-
Johns Island Presbyterian Church : its people and its community from colonial beginnings
to the twenty-first century / Charles E. Raynal.
p. cm.
Includes bibliographical references (p.).
ISBN 978-1-59629-950-4
1. Presbyterian Church (Johns Island, S.C.)--History. 2. Johns Island (S.C.)--Church history.
I. Title.
BX9211.J63R39 2010
285'.175791--dc22
2010008133

CONTENTS

PREFACE

This book tells the story of the people of Johns Island Presbyterian Church. The church is first a congregation of people who gather to worship God, to seek nurture from the resources of the Christian gospel and to come to terms with their service in response to the call of Christ. This is the story of how they came to Johns Island and built a congregation that has endured for three centuries. Their church is not simply a building or organization but a living community of faith. Their history began in the second decade of the eighteenth century and spans three centuries.

The way of life of the people of Johns Island and their churches also reflects the particular geography and location of the people of the Sea Islands of South Carolina. Therefore, to understand their way of life we must look for their part in the heritage of the South Carolina Lowcountry, to which the first European and African American immigrants came in the late 1600s. They arrived in a land where Native Americans had lived for many centuries. Many of the white settlers came to develop agriculture and reap the fruit of plantation lands obtained from the Lords Proprietors. They brought indentured servants from the British Isles and African slaves from the West Indies.

Carolina was named after Charles I, king of England; however, the life of the colony reflected a diverse cultural heritage that not only came from Western Europe but also included powerful influences from the Native

American frontier, the plantations in the Caribbean and the African customs of the slaves. The history of the people of Johns Island Presbyterian Church includes both the story of their faith and their way of life, which was born from a diverse cultural legacy.

The people survived two devastating wars and made their livings in the aftermath of both. In 1776, the colonists rose up in declaring independence from England. During the American Revolution, British soldiers of General Henry Clinton encamped near the Presbyterian meetinghouse on Johns Island, which had already been standing for a half century or more. The soldiers passed by St. John's Episcopal Church, established in 1734, on the way to Fenwick Hall, where they crossed the Stono River to James Island and joined the British siege against Charles Town. Early family memoirs indicate the upheaval and destruction on Johns Island during the War of Independence.

The Lowcountry flourished after the Revolution. According to some accounts, within eighty years the Sea Islands of South Carolina became the most prosperous region in the United States. A map sketched about 1830 by Kinsey Burden, a wealthy planter and elder in the Presbyterian Church, shows sixty-seven tracts of land on Johns Island, most of them dedicated to plantations. St. John's Episcopal Church, established in 1734, and Johns Island Presbyterian Church, established as early as 1710, with homes for their ministers, accounted for four of the sites. In 1860, the Johns Island and Wadmalaw Presbyterian congregation reported 510 slaves and 60 white members. It was the second largest Presbyterian Church in the South because it had received more African Americans into its membership than any other white congregation.

Then the Civil War laid waste to the South. Formerly well-to-do members became poor. The devastation and poverty following the Civil War lowered congregation membership. In 1862, the congregation disbanded. White members took refuge in Aiken and other parts of South Carolina, and able-bodied white men remaining in the islands joined the Stono Scouts, a Confederate militia, for reconnaissance and protection. After the war, some African American Presbyterians established Bethel, Hebron, Zion, Salem and St. Andrews Churches. These congregations are also part of the legacy of Johns Island Presbyterian Church. When the Johns Island

Presbyterian Church reassembled in 1867, about two dozen members gathered for worship, a number that remained fairly constant until the end of the nineteenth century. The church survived like Israel, wandering in the wilderness for the better part of forty years.

Recovery was slow in the twentieth century. Truck farming on smaller farms replaced cotton, which had been destroyed by the boll weevil in the 1920s. The Great Depression kept markets down until after World War II, when the economic tide rose again. In the 1970s, immigrants to the Sun Belt from other parts of the nation meant new residents and a service-oriented economy that came with the resort developments on Kiawah, Seabrook and the other Sea Islands. This late twentieth-century development continues today. The Presbyterian community on Johns Island has offered enduring and consistent worship and service not only to its own members but also to its neighbors on the islands and beyond through its mission and outreach. Its history is the story of a church that continues to make a great contribution to its neighborhood and the global community beyond; it is an important part of the history of South Carolina.

The chapters that follow tell this story in three parts, one for each of the centuries of the life of Johns Island Presbyterian Church. The first part, outlining the time from the founding of the congregation to the end of the American Revolution, relies almost entirely on secondary sources. Original documents from the period are few. In his *History of the Presbyterian Church in South Carolina*, George Howe frequently quotes contemporary old chronicles. His account of the early history is the basis for this treatment. The second part, chronicling the nineteenth century, is also dependent on Howe, but after 1855, the records of the Session of the Johns Island Presbyterian Church provide a rich source of information. The narrative comes from these records. The third part, on the twentieth century, is also based on detailed church records from the session and the church's women's organization. In the last period of the twentieth century, the history becomes an account of the remarkable way in which the pastors and members of the Johns Island church have developed an extraordinary program and ministry in response to the rapid changes that came to the area beginning in the 1970s and continue today. Throughout the account, I have relied on Erskine Clarke's *Our Southern Zion: A History of Calvinism in the South Carolina Low Country, 1690–1990.*[1]

ACKNOWLEDGEMENTS

I am grateful to many wonderful people for their help with this book. Reverend Jonathan Van Deventer, pastor of Johns Island Presbyterian Church, and the tercentenary celebration committee members—Mary Gervais Hills, chairperson—invited me to write the history of the congregation. The members of the committee have welcomed me on visits and offered good assistance. Mary Hills and Marshall Whilden (Billy) Hills, her late husband, welcomed me into their home, providing encouragement, archival material and warm hospitality. Sara Myers, director, and Chris Paton, archivist, along with other staff members of the John Bulow Campbell Library, Columbia Theological Seminary, offered continuing and cordial expert advice and access to sources. Nancy Snell Griffith, archivist, Thomason Library, Presbyterian College, Clinton, South Carolina; Paula Skreslet of the William Smith Morton Library, Union Theological Seminary and Presbyterian School of Christian Education, Richmond, Virginia; and Margery Sly and Anne Ostendarp of the Presbyterian Historical Society, Philadelphia, Pennsylvania, all happily assisted with resources. Laura All, Jaime Muehl and others at The History Press have made the preparation of the manuscript easy. Erskine Clarke, distinguished scholar of American religious history and a good friend, recommended that I take on this project and gave me good direction and valuable resources. Rosemary Alexander Raynal, my beloved wife, read the manuscript and offered expert editorial advice. My mother, Laetitia Hay Jones Raynal, to whom I dedicate this book with affection, offered room and board and wonderful conversations at her cottage at Presbyterian Village, Summerville, South Carolina. I thank them all from the bottom of my heart. Errors and omissions remain, but they are all mine.

Part I

THE EIGHTEENTH CENTURY

This part 1) presents some influences of the religious background of the Protestant Reformation on the founding of the Johns Island Presbyterian Church; 2) points out important features of colonial life in South Carolina; and 3) describes the origin of the congregation as we find it in the documents and traditions that we have today.

First, the religious heritage of the Johns Island Presbyterian Church stands on the Protestant Reformation in Western Europe. To appreciate the kind of church communities the Presbyterians built on Johns Island and elsewhere in the Charleston area, it is helpful to recognize certain aspects of Reformation belief and practices and call attention to, in particular, Puritan England and New England, from which many of the first residents came.[2]

Although the Church of England was the established church in the British colony of Carolina from 1706 until the American Revolution, Protestant theology and practice influenced the Episcopalian churches in Carolina, just as the theology of John Calvin (1509–1564) shaped that of Archbishop Thomas Cranmer in his *Book of Common Prayer* (1549) during the English Reformation. Protestant groups like the Baptists, Quakers and French Huguenots brought important ideas to early Carolina. The Huguenots were Calvinists from France, and some—especially members of the Legare family—joined and supported the Presbyterians on Johns Island. Congregationalists and Baptists from England and New England brought their own forms of Calvinism to the area. Though many of the immigrants to Carolina came mainly for the wealth of new land in the New World, the first residents wanted freedom of worship and to live by their religious convictions. Their faith and way of life played indispensable roles in the establishment of colonial South Carolina.

In the eighteenth century, the Presbyterians on Johns Island reflected this Protestant heritage. An evangelical revival began in 1730 in New England with the preaching of Jonathan Edwards (1703–1758) and spread up and down the eastern seaboard through the tireless evangelism of George Whitefield (1714–1770), a Calvinist Methodist preacher. James Oglethorpe (1696–1785) gained a royal charter in 1732 to establish the colony of Georgia. He brought John Wesley (1703–1791) and his brother, Charles (1707–1788), the most important founders of the Methodist Church, to minister to those released to Georgia from the London debtors' prisons.[3] Then Whitefield came and began his widespread preaching and efforts at social reform, including his building of the Bethesda Orphanage in Savannah. Many people hearing him professed their faith and joined churches. He preached in Charleston, as well as on James and Johns Islands. This powerful religious movement changed the shape of Christian experience for many people in established and dissenting churches. Its warm piety and religious commitments also appealed to African Americans and encouraged their religious expression.

Second, beyond the primary background of the Protestant Reformation in Europe, the particular history and character of South Carolina society play important roles throughout the history of Johns Island Presbyterian Church. In addition to ecclesiastical matters, larger social context and historical events show the story of the congregation to mirror its local setting. The founding of Carolina, stretching from Virginia into Florida, opened new land for the agricultural base of the economy that shaped the society in which the congregation was founded. Proximity to the great colonial capital city of Charleston offered access to markets and high southern culture. The character of the immigrants—especially the English, Scottish, Irish, French and Africans—made possible the establishment of a Presbyterian Church on Johns Island. The forced importation and slavery of African peoples made African Americans the majority of the population of South Carolina from the eighteenth century until the 1930s. At the end of the eighteenth century came the American Revolution. The war brought devastation to the Charleston area and disruption to life on the Sea Islands. These complex cultural and social forces and the Revolution provide historical background for the founding and life of the Johns Island Presbyterian Church in the 1700s.

Third, strong individual personalities played a formative part in the founding and development of the church. The history of the Johns Island Presbyterian community is filled with colorful characters. The founding pastor was Archibald Stobo, who escaped shipwreck in 1704 to become a Presbyterian evangelist for thirty-seven years. Thomas and James Legare, father and son, were caught in the Revolution, held on a prison ship and sent to Philadelphia. Countless ministers and members nurtured the Presbyterian community on Johns Island. Out of long-standing traditions and against the background of lived experience, remarkable people came forth and built an enduring community of Christian faith and service.

Protestant Reformation Heritage

The main religious source of the Johns Island Presbyterian Church took shape during the Protestant Reformation in sixteenth-century Europe. In the early modern period of the history of Western Europe, the central line of the Protestant Reformation began under the leadership of Martin Luther (1483–1546) in Germany. Lutheran ideas spread widely in Europe, and they influenced John Calvin when he was a theological student at the University of Paris in the 1520s. Because of the harsh repression of the Protestants by Francis I, the French monarch, Calvin fled for his life from his native France.

The Reformation had already arrived in Switzerland, and William Farel (1489–1565), the Protestant preacher in Geneva, called on John Calvin in 1538 to teach the Bible to new converts to the Reformed faith and to candidates for the Protestant ministry. Soon, Calvin was preaching several times a week and leading the organization of a new form of church and community life. Calvin built on Lutheran ideas, applying them to the second generation of the Protestant movement. Through his great contributions in teaching, preaching, biblical interpretation, theology and the constitution of the Protestant churches in Geneva, Calvin's influence spread throughout Eastern and Western Europe, especially into France, Germany, Holland and the British Isles, the countries from which the first colonial immigrants came to settle in South Carolina.

In England, Elizabeth I referred to the Calvinists as "the Reformed more reformed" because they sought to apply biblical teaching in a thorough way to individual faith and practice, as well as to church and civil government. English Puritans, Scots Presbyterians and French Huguenots had all brought their distinctive forms of Calvin's Reformed tradition to the Lowcountry by the first decade of the eighteenth century. Primarily through these groups, the Reformed influence spread more widely among the population.

In 1642, during the time of the English Civil War, Parliament ordered the writing of a new constitution for the state Church of England, to be based on Reformed theology and church polity. It was intended to replace the Anglican Church and its government by the bishops with a church organized along Puritan lines. At the behest of Parliament, an assembly of Puritan divines gathered at Westminster Cathedral in London during the seven years from 1643 to 1649. Congregational and Presbyterian representatives from England and Scotland wrote drafts and debated their statements for the proposed new Church of England. The documents that the Westminster Assembly produced were "The Directory for Public Worship," "The Form of Church Government," "The Confession of Faith," "The Larger Catechism" and "The Shorter Catechism" to replace the Anglican *Book of Common Prayer* and *The Thirty-Nine Articles*.

When Charles II returned to the monarchy in 1660, the Anglican Church was restored as the established Church of England. The work of the Westminster Assembly failed in the purpose Parliament had given it. However, adherents of the Reformation came to New England, Virginia and Carolina. The influence of "The Westminster Confession of Faith" on worship, confession, teaching and church government in the English-speaking Reformed churches was dominant for three centuries. Throughout the history of Johns Island Presbyterian Church, we can see its influence.

For example, in the eighteenth century the will of Robert Ure, a Scotsman who had come to North America in 1684, left a substantial gift of land on Johns Island to the congregation for a minister who agreed to subscribe to the Westminster Confession. At other times, the influence gave over to rejection, as in the antebellum period of the nineteenth century, when Elipha White, the pastor, and a majority of the elders of the congregation renounced the jurisdiction of the Charleston Union Presbytery. Looking ahead to recent times, in the twentieth century, the authority of the Westminster Confession and Presbyterian polity took on renewed significance in the response of the congregation to debates about Presbyterian reunion, liturgical renewal, curriculum for the church school and other practices within the denomination. At important points along the way, we can see the influence of the confession of faith's understanding of worship, confession and church practices.

After the restoration of the British monarchy in 1660, many of the English and Scottish Puritans, including Baptists, Congregationalists and Presbyterians, as well as other dissenters like the Quakers, came to the colonies in North America. Because they were deprived of the rights and privileges of the Anglican Church, they were attracted by the religious tolerance in the North American colonies, as well as the availability of land and the possibilities for a new way of life. All of these groups were influenced directly or indirectly by the Westminster Assembly. Some Baptists, Congregationalists and, especially, Presbyterians adopted and used its confession of faith, catechisms and directory for worship. The experience of independence and self-reliance and the frontier conditions of life in the North American wilderness caused not only Baptists and Congregationalists but also Presbyterians to debate the authority of Westminster orthodoxy. The American experience shaped the meaning and practices of faith traditions. The Quakers typically reacted against these beliefs and practices, and yet they shared with the Reformed tradition an emphasis on personal accountability in discipleship and simplicity in life and practices. Some Quakers, like the Stanyarnes and Hexts on Johns Island, joined the established Episcopal Church.

Erskine Clarke, in *Our Southern Zion: A History of Calvinism in the South Carolina Low Country, 1690–1990*, shows us that the Reformed community was strong and important within Lowcountry society. It brought and developed an intellectual tradition, forms of institutional life and social character that not only were recognizable in their own right but also influenced the

Episcopal Church, even though the latter had been officially established in South Carolina by the English Crown and was dominant from 1704 until the American Revolution. With the coming of more Baptists, Methodists and the Scots-Irish from about 1750 on, Calvinism gave energy and form to the broader religious and social life of South Carolina. Furthermore, many African American slaves became members of the Presbyterian churches. The slaves drew from the preaching of the gospel, colored their expression of Christian faith with their own African heritages and then gave back their distinctive contributions, embodied in worship and spiritual songs and in lives of service. After Emancipation, African Americans developed their own institutional life in their distinctive African American churches—Presbyterian, Baptist, Methodist and Episcopal. The influences of these European and African American traditions were at play in the churches in colonial Carolina and, particularly, in the Johns Island Presbyterian Church.

LIFE IN COLONIAL CAROLINA

It is helpful to consider some aspects of the well-documented history of South Carolina in the eighteenth century for the insight it can offer to an understanding of the earliest history of the congregation. What factors brought the first settlers to the Carolina Lowcountry? What forces shaped their lives? What place did religion have in their settlement?

The immediate opening for Europeans to hazard the voyage and seek to make their homes in South Carolina occurred in England. The English Civil War against the Stuart kings, led by the army of Oliver Cromwell, was unsuccessful in bequeathing a permanent new form of government to England. After Parliament declared England a commonwealth in 1649 and subsequently named Cromwell lord protector in 1653, Cromwell died in 1658. His son Richard was ill equipped to provide the strong leadership the protectorate, particularly its army, demanded. Richard Cromwell resigned in 1659, and the reprise of the commonwealth failed. Charles II, who had gone into exile, returned to the throne in 1660. To extend the rule of England as a world power and to reward those who had offered him support during his exile and brought him back to the monarchy, the king made land grants in the colonies of North America. Charles granted by royal charter a territory named Carolina to eight of his most faithful subjects. The Lords Proprietors were the Earl of Clarendon (Edward Hyde); the Duke of Albemarle (George Monck); Lord Craven; Lord Berkley; Lord Ashley (Anthony Ashley-Cooper; after 1672, Earl of Shaftesbury); Sir George Carteret; Sir William Berkley; and Sir John Colleton. All of their titles or names are place names on our map today.

The enormous grant of land, as defined in the second charter, lay between the south boundary of Virginia and a point about fifteen miles due south of today's Daytona Beach.[4] The Spanish had settled and claimed Florida for a century, and their claim extended north to include Port Royal. The terms of the charters thus rewarded the king's prominent subjects and flew in the face of the Spanish and the French, who claimed lands included in the territory of the king's grant. The Lords Proprietors offered land and freedom in generous terms to increase their own wealth and to expand the British Empire for the glory of the king and their own favor. The main attractions of Carolina to its first settlers were land and the permission to own slaves for labor. The slaves, upon whose shoulders the promised prosperity of Carolina rested, enjoyed none of the privileges of ownership or self-determination given in the Carolina charters.

The charters provided that the Anglican Church, with popular consent, could become the state church. However, the Lords Proprietors were permitted to grant liberty of worship to dissenters. Jews and even non-Christian people, including slaves and Indians, were to be left to their own religious freedom. Walter Edgar, in *South Carolina: A History*, notes that with the exception of Rhode Island, the provision for religious freedom was the most liberal in North America.[5] With this toleration, the king and the proprietors welcomed settlers from Puritan groups and other dissenters from the Anglican Church. From among them came those who had fought most fiercely against the Crown in the English Civil War. This religious toleration encouraged the founding of Baptist, Congregational, French Huguenot and Presbyterian churches whose members settled in the coastal areas of Carolina.

In 1669, Lord Ashley organized the first successful expedition to Carolina. He had it in mind to plant a colony at Port Royal, and he outfitted three ships—the *Carolina*, the *Albemarle* and the *Port Royal*, under the command of Joseph West—for the journey.[6] The three vessels arrived in Barbados in October. A storm wrecked the *Albemarle*, and it was replaced by the sloop *Three Brothers*. The *Port Royal* was wrecked in the Bahamas after six weeks of wandering off course without fresh water. The *Albemarle* was out of touch for months. Despite the losses, the storms brought good fortune in good leaders. Sir John Yeamans, a Barbados planter, accompanied the expedition to Bermuda and appointed Colonel William Sayle, an experienced colonial administrator who was seventy-nine or eighty years old at the time, as governor and commander of the ships. This early connection with the West Indies encouraged established planters to come to Carolina, providing colonists who knew the value of large grants of land, owned African slaves and could develop agricultural commerce to enrich the colony. At least four slaves came with the fleet, and others arrived soon after.[7]

When the voyagers reached sight of Port Royal in the spring of 1670, Indians, speaking broken Spanish, hailed them. The area's proximity to the Spanish, along with forbidding coastlines and inhospitable terrain, persuaded them to accept the good advice of a "very ingenious Indian," the cacique (a Spanish name for chief) of Kiawah, to settle on the banks of the Ashley River. In spite of the deaths of many of their companions on the voyage and in wrecks, by the end of May 1670 about 148 persons had settled a site of nine acres above Town Creek on the west bank of the Ashley, where the Charles Towne Landing State Park is located today. It is sheltered from view at sea by the bend of the river, the steep bank of Town Creek and marshes flooded at high tide. It required only a short palisade to protect the inland approach. The settlers named it Albemarle Point after the eldest proprietor, but the proprietors soon changed the name to Charles Towne in honor of the king.

In 1680, the town moved to is present site. At first, the settlement was on the Cooper River, between Broad and Water Streets, part of the grid on six hundred acres laid out by Governor Sayle before he died in 1671. With aggressive recruitment by the Lords Proprietors, immigrants quickly arrived, including French Huguenots and many other Protestants who were dissenters from the Church of England. Planters from Barbados continued to come. The population of Charles Towne doubled in the two years from

1680 to 1682, from 1,100 to 2,200; by 1770, the population of Charles Town had reached 5,030 whites and a majority of 5,833 blacks.[8]

Because of the policy of religious toleration, Protestant groups found welcome; they brought their faith and established churches soon after they arrived.[9] Beginning in 1680, French Huguenots came as refugees from the growing persecution after King Louis XIV (1683–1715) revoked the Edict of Nantes in 1685. (In 1598, Henry of Navarre (1553–1610), himself a Huguenot until his regency, had established the edict, a policy of toleration of Protestantism in France.) The Huguenots settled on the Santee River north of Charleston, where they established a church at Jamestown. Other Huguenots went up the east and west branches of the Cooper River and settled at Saint James Goose Creek. The largest group was in Charles Towne itself, living and working as artisans or laborers. By their gifts of ambition and achievement, Huguenots prospered as merchants and planters. They built six churches in colonial South Carolina. Soon after the proprietary laws of 1704 and 1706, which established the Episcopal Church as the official religion of the colony, all but the Huguenot Church in Charles Town merged with the Episcopal Church.

Scottish Presbyterian Covenanters seeking freedom from religious persecution came to Port Royal in 1684, where Henry Erskine (Lord Cardross), with about 150 Scots, established Stuart's Town. They were escaping the Killing Time, a bloody war between 1680 and 1688, when the Crown, under Charles II and James II, attempted to force the establishment of the Church of England on Scotland. Cardross soon returned to Scotland and then went to Holland to help William of Orange overthrow James II, the Catholic king of England, in the Glorious Revolution (1688). The Scottish colonists were diminished by the hardships of Port Royal. In the attempt to monopolize trade with the Indians, the Spanish, who claimed the territory, attacked. The colony failed. Other Scottish Presbyterians in small groups would soon come to establish Presbyterian congregations, notably one led by Archibald Stobo, the founder of Johns Island and other nearby Presbyterian churches.

In 1695, a company of New England Puritans set out for Charles Towne. They shipwrecked at Cape Fear, were rescued by the Quaker governor, John Archdale, and settled on the Wando River northwest of Charles

Towne at Cainhoy, where they organized a Presbyterian Church. A second group settled up the coast, four miles from Bull's Bay, and established the Wappetaw Independent Congregational Church. A third group from Massachusetts, with their pastor, Joseph Lord, set sail in December 1695 and came up the Ashley River to a place they named Dorchester after their towns of the same name in Massachusetts and England. They celebrated the Lord's Supper in a worship service on February 2, 1696. The colony of Georgia was founded in 1733, and in 1752 the third generation of the Dorchester Congregationalists moved to the rice-growing country in coastal Georgia. There they established Midway Congregational Church, whose large influence on Georgia and South Carolina Presbyterians would last until the Civil War.[10]

THE FOUNDING OF JOHNS ISLAND PRESBYTERIAN CHURCH

The founding of Presbyterian churches in the coastal area of South Carolina owes much to the strict and strong Scottish Presbyterian pastor Archibald Stobo. His story is remarkable. Stobo came as an evangelist from the Church of Scotland to Panama in 1698. Fifteen years after the Scottish settlement at Port Royal, Scotland again tried its hand at planting a colony; it named the colony New Caledonia. New Caledonia lay on the Isthmus of Darien (now Panama). "The Company of Scotland Trading to Africa and the Indies" attempted to establish a land bridge for commerce between the Atlantic and the Pacific. The Church of Scotland wanted to minister to the colonists and to evangelize the indigenous Indians. The Scottish Highlanders, transplanted from their homeland to the fevers of the tropics in Panama, could not tolerate the climate, and the colony failed because of starvation and disease. According to testimony from one early historian, the church mission also failed because of the overbearing preaching and the rough, non-receptive character of the Scottish colonists.[11]

The failure of the Scottish colony in Panama brought Archibald Stobo to South Carolina. The ship *Rising Sun*, on which he and his company were sailing for Scotland, was damaged in a storm off Florida, jury-

Clear glass windows, inviting the light of the sun, are a typical feature of church meetinghouses built under the influence of the English Puritan Reformation. *Photograph by Katharine Bair.*

rigged and at last set anchor in Charles Town Harbor. The congregation of the Independent Meetinghouse called him ashore for pastoral services. According to one story, he was summoned to perform the marriage service. A hurricane blew in while he and his wife were in Charleston, destroying the ship and drowning its crew and passengers. The church was at the time also called "the Presbyterian Church"; later, with a new building, it became "the White Meeting" and still later, the "Circular Congregational Church."

That the Congregational Church should call a Presbyterian minister confirms that the relationships among the various branches of the Reformed tradition in the Charles Town area at the beginning of the eighteenth century

This Bible belonged to Archibald Stobo, founder of Johns Island Presbyterian Church in the early eighteenth century. *Used by permission of the South Carolina Historical Society, Charleston, South Carolina.*

were open and fluid. The demands of organizing congregations in this harsh time urged cooperation and made some religious controversies seem irrelevant. Furthermore, all of these Reformed Protestants had escaped fierce religious persecution, and under the circumstances they had little to gain from intolerance in the family of their faith. These factors fell in easily with the Lords Proprietors' promised tolerance in religion and wish to encourage many and diverse groups of immigrants to come to South Carolina. As we shall see, such good relations would not always prevail within the Christian churches in the coming years.

The memory that Stobo was a commanding presence and fulsome preacher is preserved in a history of the Legare family. Eliza C. Fludd, recounting early stories from her Legare ancestors, writes, "As soon as Mr. Stobo was installed as pastor of the Church, he began to urge the congregation to unite…with the Presbyterian Church of Scotland. This the French and English elements positively and decidedly refused to do."[12]

In a reference to her ancestor, Solomon Legaré, a Huguenot who had come to Charles Towne in 1697, Fludd offers insight into another strong personality whose family would also soon leave its mark on the Johns Island Presbyterian Church:

> *Mr. Legaré was strict in the observance of regular hours, and to his great annoyance, the Rev. Mr. Stobo, who preached at one time in the Congregational church, gave sermons of such unusual length that they often interfered with the dinner hour. At length Mr. Legaré was determined to submit no longer to such irregularity; and the next Sabbath he got up with his family in the midst of the discourse and was about to leave the church, when the Rev. Scotch gentleman, perceiving his intention called out from the pulpit: "Aye, ay, a little pitcher is soon full!" Upon which irreverent address, the Huguenot's French blood became excited, and turning himself about in the middle of the aisle, he still more irreverently, and not altogether to his credit, retorted, "And you are an old fool!" He then quietly went home with his family, ate his dinner, returned with them to the church, and then listened to the balance of the discourse as gravely as if nothing unusual had occurred.*[13]

In 1704, Stobo left Independent Meetinghouse, which called upon the Reverend William Livingston, an Irish immigrant from New England, to succeed him. Further, "Mr. Stobo was [in 1710–20] exercising his ministerial gifts wherever his labors were most needed in the colony."[14] George Howe, in his history of the Presbyterian Church in South Carolina, cites a letter from Charles Town, written June 1, 1710, which says that there were "five churches of British Presbyterians" in the area.[15] So it is possible that the three Presbyterian churches on Edisto Island, James Island and Johns Island had been founded by 1710. One of the five was the Independent Meetinghouse. Cainhoy Presbyterian Church in what is now Berkley County was probably another. Later in the same early period, Stobo founded "on the Presbyterian plan" churches at Wilton and Bethel Church on Pon Pon, near Walterboro.[16]

Alexander Hewat (ca. 1740–1828), the pastor of the (Scots) Presbyterian Church from 1763 to 1770, had published in London a history of South Carolina, *An Historical Account of the Rise and Progress of the Colonies of South Carolina and Georgia.*[17] In it he declared that at the time of the formation of the presbytery (about 1728), Presbyterian churches had already been established "in three of the maritime islands." From these bits of information, Howe concludes, "The Presbyterian Church on Johns Island must have existed as early as 1720, if not before."[18] To the best of our knowledge, the churches on James Island, Edisto Island and Johns Island were founded about the same time in the second decade of the eighteenth century. We lack documents to specify the dates more precisely.

By 1730, Stobo, along with ministers John Witherspoon of James Island, Hugh Fisher of Dorchester, Nathan Basset of Charles Town and Josiah Smith of Cainhoy, had formed a presbytery made up of ministers and lay elders elected as commissioners from the congregations. It was the third presbytery to be formed in the colonies, following those in New York and Philadelphia. It was called by various names: "Presbytery of the Province," "Presbytery of South Carolina" and "Presbytery of Charlestown." John Fisher, pastor of the Congregational Church at Wando Neck, was listed as a non-subscribing member.[19] Subscription was the requirement that Presbyterian officers, both pastors and elected lay elders, accept the Westminster Confession as the confessional standard for ordination in the Presbyterian Church. Congregational ministers sat with the presbytery without subscribing. The presbytery that they founded was a loose association of Presbyterian and Congregational members not connected with any other association, but they debated issues that led to the formation of early denominational and confessional identity in the colonies.

In 1728, the Presbyterian Synod of Philadelphia passed "the Adopting Act," which required subscription to the Westminster Confession, excepting its statement on the powers of the civil magistrate, which referred to the political circumstances of its composition in England in the 1640s. To require subscription to a confession of faith was a controversial action among different strands of the Reformed tradition. Some held that to adopt the Westminster Confession and the Westminster catechisms made these creedal statements equal in authority to the Bible. Others argued that the documents were subordinate to the Scriptures and reliable guides to faith and practice. The debate came before the South Carolina Presbytery formed by Archibald Stobo and his colleagues.

In 1724, Nathan Bassett became pastor of the Independent Meetinghouse in Charles Town (at this time still frequently called the "Presbyterian Church"). Josiah Smith, the son of the governor of the colony (1693), was born in Charles Town in 1704, graduated from Harvard College in 1725, was a minister in Bermuda for a time and came to Cainhoy Presbyterian Church about 1728. Bassett and Smith, though participating in the presbytery, were firmly congregational in their views about church government, and both opposed any requirement of subscription to the Westminster Assembly documents.

Smith published a sermon in 1729 titled "Human Impositions proved unscriptural; or, the Divine Right of Private Judgment," which opposed requiring members to subscribe to the Westminster documents. Hugh Fisher, of the Dorchester Congregational Church, argued for subscription, and he answered Smith with "A Preservative against Dangerous Errors in the Unction of the Holy One." Smith probably left the presbytery, but the controversy continued and brought separation.

The Independent Meetinghouse congregation included both Presbyterians and Independents, but in 1731 the Presbyterians separated and formed First (Scots) Presbyterian Church according to the model of the Church of Scotland. Archibald Stobo, who according to an early observer was "strongly attached to the Presbyterian form of government," probably had a hand in the Scottish exodus from the Congregational meeting. Perhaps his short tenure as pastor of Johns Island Presbyterian Church ended in 1704 because of the controversy his strict Presbyterian convictions caused among the independent-minded planters on the island. We cannot be sure. However, despite the loyalty of some members to the Westminster Confession and Presbyterian form of government, this early presbytery remained independent and never became connected to another regional governing body of Presbyterian churches. It ceased to meet after the beginning of the American Revolution.

One of the last words on record about Archibald Stobo's ministry concerns the response of his congregation at Wilton when members learned during worship on Sunday, September 9, 1739, of a slave rebellion that had occurred nearby. The rebellious slaves had gathered on the west branch of the Stono River on the night of September 8, moved to the Stono bridge, stolen guns and ammunition from a store, killed five whites, burned a house and then gone southward, aiming to get to Florida, where the Spanish government promised freedom to any slave. On the way, they reached a tavern and spared the innkeeper but slaughtered his neighbors and burned four houses. As they marched with drums and banners, Lieutenant Governor William Bull (1683–1755), returning to Charles Town with four other men, came by chance upon the rally of sixty to one hundred slaves who had stopped near the South Edisto River not far from the Wilton Presbyterian Church, where morning worship was going on.

Alexander Hewat, perhaps because he was a friend of Governor William Bull Jr., whose father encountered the Stono revolt, records particular details of the event:

> *Governor Bull returning to Charlestown from the southward, met them, and, observing them armed, quickly rode out of their way. He spread the alarm, which soon reached the Presbyterian church at Wiltown, where Archibald Stobo was preaching to a numerous congregation of planters in that quarter. By a law of the province all planters were obliged to carry their arms to church, which at this critical juncture proved a very useful and necessary regulation. The women were left in church trembling with*

fear, while the militia, under the command of Captain Bee, marched in quest of the negroes, who by this time had become formidable from the number that joined them. They had marched above twelve miles and spread desolation through all the plantations in their way. Having found rum in some houses and drunk freely of it, they halted in an open field and began to sing and dance by way of triumph. During these rejoicings the militia discovered them, and stationed themselves in different places around them to prevent them from making their escape. The intoxication of several of the slaves favoured the assailants. One party advanced into the open field and attacked them, and, having killed some negroes, the remainder took to the woods and were dispersed. Many ran back to their plantations in hopes of escaping suspicion from the absence of their masters, but the greater part were taken and tried. Such as had been compelled to join them contrary to their inclination were pardoned, but all the chosen leaders and first insurgents suffered death.[20]

Howe attributes the Stono Rebellion to two factors.[21] The first was the continuing strife between Spain and England. Spain had claimed Florida up to Port Royal for a century. The Spanish had encouraged the Yemassee Indians to attack the colonists, and the Yemassee War (1715) brought mayhem to the coastal area.[22] In the next decades, Spain summoned the Creek tribe and free blacks to turn against Georgia. Slaves in South Carolina who stole away to the Spanish were given freedom. So, by Howe's reckoning, the Stono slaves were pawns in this colonial rivalry between Spain and England. Secondly, Howe attributes the rebellion to slaves "who had not yet lost the fierceness of their savage state." He meant that the importation from Africa brought wild and uncivilized new slaves who had not learned the submission and obedience that plantation labor required. Howe was writing in the decades immediately before and after the Civil War. In 1870, when his book was published, he avoided questioning the institution of slavery itself. Today, it is easier for us to recognize its cruelties and injustice.

Archibald Stobo died sometime in 1741. He had served as pastor for forty years. During the course of his ministry, he served or founded at least four and possibly six churches. He played an important role on Johns Island in the Presbyterian Church. He helped establish a presbytery that supported the pastors and congregations. He was a remarkable leader in the Reformed churches of the Lowcountry in the years of the settlement of South Carolina.

A few details from the story of Johns Island Presbyterian Church emerge from the period leading up to the American War of Independence. According to one record, Johns Island "enjoyed the ministerial services of The Rev. Mr. Turnbull" after 1730. Perhaps he came earlier. During his ministry in 1735, the church received a valuable legacy worth about £3,656 from Robert Ure, a Scottish resident of Johns Island, in the form of a designated trust specified in the following words:

> *For the maintenance of a minister of the gospel, according to the Presbyterian profession, who is, or shall be thereafter, from time to time regularly called and settled on Johns Island, in Colleton county, in said province, and who shall acknowledge and subscribe the Westminster Confession of Faith as the confession of his faith, and shall firmly believe and preach the same to the people there committed, or which shall hereafter be committed to his care and pastoral inspection.*[23]

Ure's devotion to the Westminster Confession is consistent with Scottish Presbyterianism and the fervent conviction of Archibald Stobo. Furthermore, we have in this will indication that Johns Island was a welcoming dwelling place for residents who were attracted to the island and its Presbyterian church. Perhaps it was Ure's legacy that helped build the magnificent Presbyterian meetinghouse on Johns Island. Even though local tradition in the church says it was constructed in 1719, it seems at least as likely that Ure's legacy funded the meetinghouse.

The meetinghouse's architectural design reflects the craft, tastes and even character of life of eighteenth-century Reformed Protestant Christians. It was built out of lumber harvested on the island or brought from nearby via waterways. The carpentry was done by skilled slaves who sawed the lumber from timbers. The flooring and molded panels of the pews and wainscoting are of pine and cypress. In the roof construction, kingpost trusses support the rafters, which are mortise and tenon pinned with pegs. The original roof shingles were rived from cypress logs and were durable enough to last until after the Civil War, well over a century later. The ceiling was plaster on lathe, embossed with a large sunflower; it was destroyed in 1886 by the great Charleston earthquake and replaced with wood. The foundation bricks came as ballast in English ships, and the risers of the steps on the sides were covered with Italian marble. The gallery and other additions were built in 1823, when Elipha White was minister.

At a later time, the slaves who came to worship entered through the doors by the narrow gallery stairs on either side of the gable end facing southeast toward today's Bohicket Road. The high gables above are adorned with wooden fans. The pew boxes, rented to support the pastor, face a pulpit nine feet high, focusing the attention of the worshipers to the reading of the Bible and the sermon. A table in the front was moved and set for quarterly Communion, during which the white members and, after them, the slave members from the gallery came forward for the Lord's Supper. Baptismal water for sprinkling infants or adults was brought in a pitcher. Illumination was mainly by the light of the sun shining through the clear glass windows, augmented by candles and later by oil lamps. The plain, simple design, full of light, focused on the Word and sacraments, emphasizing the accessibility of the gospel of Jesus Christ to all who could hear it preached and join the celebration of the sacraments. The architecture reflected the conviction that the Bible, when read and faithfully interpreted in the hearing of the people, could bring them to faith and motivate them to live as servants of Jesus Christ. To this day, the Presbyterian meetinghouse on Johns Island is a simple, elegant place of worship. Its architecture points us to the life of the people of faith who built the meetinghouse as a space to gather together seeking and expressing their faith in God.

After Turnbull died, the Reverend Thomas Murray came in 1737, and he remained the pastor until his death in 1753, an unusually long pastorate of sixteen years for the Johns Island church. Although we do not have records from his pastorate, a fascinating detail suggests that Johns Island was not isolated but deeply engaged with the cultural influences of Charles Town and the wider colonial world. During Murray's pastorate, we find that George Whitefield preached at Johns Island.

Whitefield, a minister from Gloucester, England, was associated with John and Charles Wesley in the revival within the Anglican Church that led to the establishment of Methodism. Whitefield, like the Wesley brothers, came

The restoration of the pulpit to its original form was an important part of the renovation of the historic design of the sanctuary. *Photograph by Katharine Bair.*

to Georgia and South Carolina. He traveled from New York to Georgia on the eastern seaboard, preaching and raising money for Bethesda House, an orphanage to be built in Savannah. Whitefield and Jonathan Edwards, the great Congregational missionary, preacher and theologian in New England, were leading preachers of the evangelical revival in the colonies called the Great Awakening. In 1738, the commissary of the bishop of London, Reverend Alexander Garden, minister at St. Philips Church in Charles Town, welcomed Whitefield to the pulpit. However, when Whitefield returned to Charles Town in 1740, Commissary Garden, on orders from London, suspended him from the ministry. Neither the controversy nor the suspension deterred Whitefield.

Not only did the Methodist Church come as part of the Great Awakening, but the revival also had a lively influence on the Congregational and Presbyterian Churches. It provided a form of religious expression and piety that brought self-examination and a deeply personal religious commitment to many people within the churches, as well as to many who had no relationship to any church. Whitefield's influence touched the congregations at the Independent Meetinghouse, the French Huguenot Church, the Baptist

Church, First (Scots) Presbyterian Church and the Dorchester Congregational Church, as well as the Presbyterian Church on James Island and Bethel Pon Pon on the South Edisto River. As a result of the Great Awakening, churches began to grow in membership. Whitefield advocated that the white churches preach and teach Christianity to the slaves. Whitefield's preaching and evangelical work brought renewal to many people in Reformed churches. Its emphasis on the affections of the human heart opened Christianity to African Americans in a powerful way.[24]

Whitefield's preaching in the Independent Meetinghouse in Charles Town awakened evangelical faith in the household of Thomas Legare Sr., one of the most important members and early supporters of the Johns Island Presbyterian Church. The Legare family remembered that it was through Mrs. Legare, Eliza Basnett, that the influence of Whitefield's preaching had such strong effect. She was the daughter of Mr. John Basnett, the counselor of King George III for the chancery courts. Basnett was a deist, like many intellectuals of the Enlightenment period in England, Scotland and North America. The Basnetts and Legares attended the Congregational Independent Meetinghouse. Eliza Basnett was moved by Whitefield's preaching. Both she and Thomas Legare adopted the commitments of the faith. They entertained Whitefield in their homes in Charles Town and Johns Island when he preached there and on James Island in 1740.[25]

Thomas Murray was the Presbyterian pastor on Johns Island at the time. We have no record of his convictions about the Great Awakening. However, through the Legare family, the impact of the new emphasis on the personal experience of faith was bound to have had a significant influence. It would have been a different religious temperament from the strict Scottish Calvinism of Stobo and Robert Ure, the generous benefactor of the church, and would have moderated its emphasis on predestination and the eternal decrees of God in favor of a more personal response to God's grace. Certainly, over the next decades the members and ministers of Johns Island Presbyterian Church warmly embraced the call to bring slave members into the church until it enfolded more slave members than any other Presbyterian congregation except Zion Presbyterian Church in Charles Town. This evangelical commitment was one of the gifts of the Great Awakening to the Johns Island Presbyterian Church.

We do have indication of the nature of Murray's pastoral leadership from the notice of his death in August 1753:

> *Died, revd Thos. Murray, minister on Johns Island, universally lamented. As his ministerial habits, cheerful conversation, steady friendship, and unaffected piety commanded the respect and engaged the affections of all that knew him, his death is not only a particular but a public loss.*[26]

In April 1755, the Reverend Charles Lorimer was installed as pastor, having resigned his pastorate at the Scots Presbyterian Church in Charles Town in April 1755, seven months earlier. Archibald Simpson, pastor of Stoney Creek in Yemassee ("the Indian Land") and founder of Saltketcher Church northwest of Walterboro in 1766, records in his journal the unhappiness at First (Scots) Presbyterian Church. "Mr. Lorimer, about three years ago (1751), was most cried up and esteemed, but is not able now to continue his ministry with any comfort and satisfaction."[27] Perhaps the people of Johns Island were more receptive to him. The *South Carolina Gazette* reported that he left for England nine years later on July 8, 1764.[28]

In 1765, the South Carolina legislature approved the purchase of 212 acres of land from Robert Turner by Joseph Stanyarne, James Carson, John Freer, Henry Livingston and Hugh Wilson "for the use of the pastor or minister of the meeting-house on Johns' Island, as a glebe or parsonage."[29] The Reverend James Latta began his ministry on Johns Island in 1768. He married Sarah, the daughter of Hugh Wilson, on March 24, 1775. The succession of pastors during these years before and after the Revolution is not complete, and we do not know when Latta's ministry ended. Perhaps his departure was caused by the Revolution.

The strategic importance of Charles Town for the American colonies, and subsequently for the imperial aims of Great Britain, brought conflict to the South Carolina Lowcountry both early and late in the American Revolution. Early in the war, a naval battle occurred in Charles Town Harbor on November 11–12, 1775, and on June 28, 1776, while the Continental Congress meeting in Philadelphia was debating the Declaration of Independence, Fort Moultrie came under attack. After the fall of Savannah in 1778, the British general Augustine Prevost invaded South Carolina, engaging Captain

William Moultrie's troops in Charles Town. Lord Clinton—commanding a British southern strategy and invading with the largest British force in any battle of the Revolution except at Philadelphia—came ashore on Simmons (Seabrook) Island in February 1780, crossed Johns Island, James Island and the Ashley River and reached the mainland.

The bombardment of Charles Town began in April. Clinton seized all avenues of escape. Fort Moultrie surrendered, and General Benjamin Lincoln surrendered the city on May 12. Clinton's army captured over five thousand Patriots and confiscated all public property. The Continental soldiers were held, some in ships in the harbor. Militia members were paroled, upon threat of execution, to their homes or plantations. British officers were billeted in homes. Amidst the destruction and chaos, British soldiers plundered private property. Slaves, promised freedom, flocked to the British; vast numbers were shipped to the West Indies and sold again as slaves. Many died of starvation and disease.

In the path of this tumult, Johns Island suffered the high cost of war. In part, the conflict was civil, pitting neighbor against neighbor. Many citizens of colonial Carolina were Tories and doubted the wisdom or even viability of independence from Great Britain. Most of the planters in the Episcopal and Reformed Churches supported the War of Independence. Thomas Legare, member and supporter of both the Independent Meetinghouse (Congregational) in Charles Town and Johns Island Presbyterian Church, along with William Hext of St. Johns Episcopal Church, organized and trained a militia company of seventy or eighty men. Edward and Thomas Fenwick, sons of one of the earliest English settlers, trained with the St. John's militia, but on June 30, 1779, Thomas Fenwick led a British detachment to the night camp under command of John Raven Mathews at Ravenwood Plantation, where they killed or captured virtually the whole militia. In 1780, Fenwick Hall became a rallying point for Lord Clinton and Lord Cornwallis in the British march toward Charles Town. Cornwallis's regulars, on their overland march from Simmons Island, gathered at the Presbyterian church.

Thomas Legare the elder went as a parolee with his family to his plantation in Monck's Corner, but the plantation was plundered by Lieutenant Colonel Banastre Tarleton's troops. Moving again to Charles Town, Legare found his family lodging in the upper story of a house with British soldiers on the first floor. He was imprisoned in the Provost Prison along with Dr. Ramsey, a prominent fellow church member at the Independent Meetinghouse in Charles Town. The elder Thomas's sons, Thomas and James Legare, and John B. Holmes, also from Johns Island, were imprisoned on board a ship in Charles Town Harbor and were sent to Philadelphia. Finally, as Cornwallis was forced into Virginia and to his ultimate surrender at Yorktown (October 1781), Thomas and James Legare, in a harrowing trip by foot and horseback, came back to join their family, only to discover that they, too, had been sent to Philadelphia. The two men returned to that city to meet them and bring them back home.

What should we make of these family recollections of the Revolutionary period? They illustrate the savagery of warfare, which came home to the people of Johns Island. We also have a record of the fierce and determined independence of prominent members of the churches on the island. The Legare family paid a high price for embracing the cause for independence of the colonies from England. The reasons for their devotion were complex. Two generations previously, Solomon Legare had come as a Huguenot, escaping religious persecution. In time, the family acquired property and wealth. They were loath to surrender their fortune to imperial Britain. Furthermore, they were heirs of the Reformation theology of John Calvin, who considered civil government a gift of God for the well-being of the community and believed it deserved the loyalty and service of its citizens. This high view of civil government led Calvin's followers to demand justice and accountability in civil leadership, and it also led some of them to overthrow tyrannical rulers by force.

Part II

THE NINETEENTH CENTURY

The story of the Johns Island and Wadmalaw Presbyterian Church in the nineteenth century is remarkable for the way the church reflected and responded to the great historical events in which it participated and because of the colorful pastors and church members who left us their testimonies. This part has three sections that reflect the changing life of the church during the nineteenth century: 1) the first fifty years, from the late 1700s through the pastorate of Elipha White (1822–49); 2) from 1850 to the end of the Civil War; and 3) the recovery of the congregation after the war from 1867 to 1898. In each of these sections, we can see the influences of the congregation's historical context and how the pastors and members worked out their own responses in Christian faith.

THE FIRST FIFTY YEARS

During the Revolution, the British took Charles Town, confined many to prison ships, restored the former royal governor and launched their drive toward the west and north through the Carolinas. The Sea Islands were the origin of their route of attack. After the surrender of Lord Cornwallis at Yorktown on October 19, 1781, South Carolina engaged in a time of rebuilding that lasted through the first decade of the nineteenth century.

According to some scholars, by the end of the colonial period, the Lowcountry of South Carolina had achieved the greatest wealth of anywhere in the United States.[30]

The economic depression caused by the second war with England in 1812 yielded to the restoration of high profits in the rice and cotton markets. These products brought to an elite group wealth that few Americans had ever known. Plantation owners claimed a social prestige that equaled, if it did not surpass, any other group in North America. This upward economic climb stood on the shoulders of the African American slaves, who numbered more than twice the white population in the Lowcountry by the time the Civil War began in the Charleston Harbor in 1861.

On the national scene, South Carolina legislator John C. Calhoun (1780–1850) became vice president under John Quincy Adams (1825–29) and remained so for a time under Andrew Jackson, the seventh president. Calhoun resigned in 1832 and became a U.S. senator. He was the most prominent public leader from South Carolina in the first half of the century, and he is most famous for authoring the rationale for nullification.[31] Written in a determined reaction against national tariffs designed to protect manufactured goods and raw materials, Calhoun's doctrine said that since the states had given authority to the United States Constitution, they had the right, by vote in convention, to nullify any statute enacted by Congress.

During the 1830s, South Carolina, more than any other state, was divided between nullifiers, who called for the repeal of the tariffs, and unionists, who were more moderate and urged working under the authority of the Constitution. A compromise in 1833 ended the debate about the tariff after President Jackson declared it incompatible with the Union, but the destructive outcome lingered. This debate came during the ministry of Reverend Elipha White, who came to Johns Island in 1822, and it influenced the decision of the congregation to secede from the Presbyterian Church.

In religion, an evangelical uplift came in the form of the Second Great Awakening, a movement of revivals on the eastern seaboard and westward into the backcountry. These began in New England, particularly under the leadership of Congregational teacher Timothy Dwight IV (1752–1817) at Yale.[32] In Boston, Andover Seminary was founded in 1807 to educate a new generation of Congregational ministers and missionaries, many of whom would come south as evangelists to preach and organize churches. Elipha White came to Johns Island because of this revival. Benevolent societies for education and mission, both domestic and foreign, began to unite Protestants in common support for teaching and supplying ministers, missionaries and the publication of the Bible and religious literature. The revival brought to the South the conviction that African Americans should be evangelized, taught the Christian faith and incorporated into the white churches. The influence of these new commitments came home to the Johns Island churches, both Presbyterian and Episcopal.

After the British left Charles Town at the end of the Revolution, the great port city sought a renewal. In 1783, it changed its name to "Charleston" and claimed to be "the capital of the South." Johns Island residents also had to seek a new way forward. Both the Presbyterian and Episcopal Churches on Johns Island undertook the task of rebuilding and ministering to the community after the war. The Johns Island Presbyterian Church was incorporated by the South Carolina legislature in 1785; this charter gave it legal standing and the right to own property. The congregation appealed through Congregational and Presbyterian connections for pastors, and several supply ministers served the Johns Island Presbyterian Church.

Around 1793 or 1794, a church was built on Wadmalaw to "unite that people with Johns Island in the support of the gospel, since which the style of the church has been 'The Presbyterian church of John's Island and Wadmalaw.'"[33] The ministers served both congregations. A series of supply ministers served for short periods during the last years of the 1700s: James Templeton (1792), Robert Wilson, S.W. Yongue, D.E. Dunlap, Mr. Montgomery, Mr. Gilleand, Andrew Brown, Moses Waddell and James W. Stephenson (1793–97). Finally, in 1800 Mr. James McElhenny accepted the call of the congregation, but in April he sent a letter resigning his pastoral charge, and the Presbytery of South Carolina released him because of "want of Harmony between the parties."[34] The cause of the disagreement is unknown, but for five more years the congregation had no regular pastor.

It was not until 1806 that Dr. William Clarkson accepted its call, and fortunately Dr. Clarkson was able to serve for six years. Clarkson received his MD from the University of Pennsylvania in 1785. He married Kitty Floyd of Long Island, New York, daughter of General William Floyd, a signer

The Reverend William Clarkson came to the Johns Island Presbyterian Church in 1806 and served until he died in 1812. He was a physician before he became a minister and moved to the South from New York. *Archives of Johns Island Presbyterian Church.*

of the Declaration of Independence. Because of ill health, he gave up the practice of medicine and became a Presbyterian minister, serving in New Jersey, New York and Savannah and on Johns Island. His ministry was cut short when he died in 1812.[35]

Clarkson's is the oldest grave in the churchyard. His stone reads:

In memory of the Rev. Wm. Clarkson

Who, during the last six years of his life, sustained the pastoral charge of the united Presbyterian Churches on this Island and on Wadmalaw. And while zealously discharging the important duties of his ministry, was by a short illness summoned from his useful labors to enter into the joy of his Lord on the 9th day of September, 1812, and in the 50th year of his age. He was a native of Philadelphia and of very respectable parentage and connexions [sic]. As a husband, a father, a friend, and in the various relations of his life, he exhibited an amiable example of affection, tenderness, and Christian integrity in his public character and service. As a minister of Christ,

"I would express him, simple, grave, sincere,
In doctrine uncorrupt: in language plain,
And plain in manner-----------
--------------------Much impressed
Himself, as conscious of his awful charge,
And anxious mainly that the flock he fed
Might feel it too: affectionate in look
And tender in address, as well became
A messenger of grace to guilty men.
For him to live was Christ, to die was gain." [36]

The praise of the minister as "conscious of his awful charge" meant that he conducted his work with the awe appropriate to the service of God, but at least one of his hearers found Clarkson's preaching harsh. Ichabod Brewster, a physician on Johns Island, was also originally from New England. In a letter to his brother in Hartford, Brewster mentioned Clarkson: "Our minister here is Presbyterian, who preaches on both the Islands on alternate Sundays. Fire and brimstone! His congregation is thin."[37] Perhaps his vigorous preaching was one characteristic of the revival of religion going on at the time. The thinness of the congregation meant that not many members attended worship. Perhaps fewer than two dozen members belonged to the church. In the winters, many of the members who had homes in Charleston might have been in the city and attended worship in churches there. Some were members of a church in the city and a church near their plantations. After Clarkson's death in 1812, the congregations on Johns and Wadmalaw Islands were again served for short terms.

The letters between Ichabod and Anson Brewster give interesting insights into life on Johns Island in the early nineteenth century. Ichabod writes to his farmer brother in New England, "There is no sale for cotton at present. Long staple on Sea Island is held at 20 cents, and short staple or green seed at 9 cents per lb." He writes of the threat of war in 1813, "It was the theatre of bloodshed during the revolution; I suspect that ere long we shall feel the evils of war, if this contest continues. The famous battle of Stono was fought within five miles of where I live." He adds the feeling of danger:

William Clarkson's gravestone is the oldest in the cemetery. *Photograph by Katharine Bair.*

View the defenseless situation of this State—A servile enemy among us—a scattered population—and an undisciplined militia—take all this into consideration and you will have no reason to think that I live retired, or at any rate, secure "from the din of War!" At all events, should the British relinquish the contest in Spain, and making a landing in east Florida, Georgia and Carolina would then have sufficient proof that we were really at war.

"The servile enemy" referred to the threat of slave uprising, and Brewster's mention of it speaks of a continuing anxiety that pervaded the Charleston area. The threat of the British, recalling the Revolution and fearing another invasion on the coast, never materialized. His reaction to the threat from England shows the fear on the island of a second war. Even though the islands escaped invasion, the effects of the War of 1812 came in the form of economic depression in cotton and rice exports.

Ichabod Brewster died in September 1813.[38] His brother made the journey from Hartford to Johns Island to settle the estate, and his letter gives a firsthand account of the churchyard and some aspects of life on the island.[39] Anson describes visiting the grave, the second oldest in the cemetery. His description is at first a melancholy reflection:

> *I visited the melancholy spot where Ichabod is buried two days after I wrote you my last letter. It is impossible to convey to you any idea of my feelings when I come to his grave—there his body lies alone! In the woods, distant from any house, excepting a Meetinghouse—his grave is at the foot of a large walnut tree, covered from the top to bottom with long moss peculiar to this climate which hangs to the ground. All the other trees around this are thus covered likewise. The whole picture is gloom beyond description. It looks like the valley of death.*

Then his mood of grief passes, and he writes about the climate and the food crops:

> *Some days it is very warm indeed—I have seen several orange trees hanging full of oranges. The fig tree is yet green. They are planting peas, radishes, &c—we have excellent head lettuce every day—it is growing green in the gardens—and the rose bush is full of full blown roses—but notwithstanding all these things I wish I was on my way to you.*

These words of the grieving brother of a member of Johns Island and Wadmalaw Church give us a sense of the time and character of the place. The family came from New England like many others in the early nineteenth century. Dr. Ichabod Brewster was the first of a long line of physicians on whom the residents relied. However, life was precarious and frequently cut short, as in Clarkson's and Brewster's cases. England was still a threat to the new nation and caused worry in the coastal area. Slaves were necessary for the plantation economy, but white people feared rebellion. The isolated churchyard and the drooping Spanish moss created a somber mood. Yet the land was fruitful for growing food and marketable crops for a good life. Sea Island cotton was especially important, though for the moment the market was low.

Again a series of supply preachers filled the pulpit from 1812 to 1821.[40] Mr. Morse came after Clarkson. In 1814, the congregation appealed to

Harmony Presbytery to be taken under its care. The church was vacant until Mr. John Cruickshanks, a licensed Presbyterian minister from New Brunswick Presbytery, New Jersey, was called in April 1816. He served two years until his death. Again the church was vacant; it was served occasionally by Mr. Abbott, Mr. Wright and Mr. Richard Cary Morse. The sporadic service of ministers tells us that in those years the congregation was isolated and was not able to attract the service of full-time pastors. However, with the increasing prosperity of the islands, the church sought to call a full-time pastor.

The long period of short interims came to end with the call to Elipha White. This capable man led the congregation in a formative way from 1822 until his death in 1849. He influenced the character of the congregation as it developed through the years. Born on October 8, 1795, in East Randolph, Massachusetts, White graduated from Brown University in 1817 and from Andover Seminary in 1820. Andover Seminary was founded in 1807 in Massachusetts by a group of moderate evangelical Calvinists associated with the Second Great Awakening in New England. Since Reformed churches in the West and the South needed pastors, the Presbyterian and Congregational denominations, working cooperatively under the Plan of Union (1801), sent missionary pastors. White was committed to this evangelical Calvinism. He became a candidate of the Congregational Missionary Society of South Carolina and was ordained at the Circular Congregational Church in Charleston in January 1821.

Johns Island was considered a home mission field. White transferred from the Congregational denomination, became a member of Harmony Presbytery and received a call from the Johns Island church on April 20, 1822. He married Elizabeth Legare, daughter of the younger Thomas Legare (1766–1838).[41] They had a daughter, Susan, who died at age seven in 1828.[42] His influence as a pastor in the Charleston area came in part from his marriage into the Legare family, which gave him prominent connections in Charleston and on Johns Island.

In addition to being well connected, White had great personal gifts. Beyond the Johns Island congregation, his oratory skill brought him invitations from the educational and mission societies in New England and Charleston. While he was minister on Johns Island, ten of his sermons and addresses were published in Charleston, Boston and Indianapolis, places where he spoke. He was a member of the American Education Society and gave the "Introductory Discourse" before the American Institute of Instruction in Worcester, Massachusetts, in 1837. These two benevolent societies developed and contributed to education for ministers and public education in North America.[43]

White had a forceful, tenacious personality, revealed in his leadership in Charleston Union Presbytery, which he joined at the time of its founding in 1822. He was outspoken at two Presbyterian General Assemblies in 1837 and 1838. He attracted the attention of radical abolitionists in the North because he was a former New England Congregational minister who defended slavery and perhaps owned one or more slaves.[44] In 1838, he and the majority of the session rejected any tie with the presbytery and led the congregation to declare independence from the Presbyterians and all other denominations. For twenty-seven years, at home and in wider church circles, he was a forceful and decisive leader.[45] In 1849, at age fifty-four, he died following a fall from horseback.[46] He served the longest term of any pastor in the history of the Johns Island Presbyterian Church.

The memorials to White in the cemetery and sanctuary confirm the congregation's great affection for him. In his epitaph are the following words:

> *Endowed with qualities which in the domestic and social circles, elicited the tenderest affections, and proved attractive of the sincerest friendship; commanding respect in general society, alike by the force of his intellect, the elevation of his sentiments, and the dignified amenity of his manners; in all that pertained to principle—characterized by the most inflexible firmness; gifted with an impressive eloquence; exhibiting in all the relations of life the marked characteristics of a Puritan ancestry; his talents and his influence, he laid upon the altar of his God, serving him in the Gospel.*[47]

The eulogy, in high rhetoric, celebrates his home and social ties. His intellect, strong sentiments and dignity inspired respect in society. He was a person of high moral and personal standards. He brought prestige and strength to the congregation, and they loved him for it.

The economy of South Carolina began to grow while White was minister. It gave strength to the congregation, which rode the rising tide brought by the expansion of the rice and cotton markets, particularly long staple Sea Island cotton. During White's pastorate, the ruling elders were Kinsey Burden, clerk of session, one of the wealthiest and best-known planters on the Sea Islands; Thomas Legare, the pastor's father-in-law; and Hugh Wilson. All three planters held large resources of land and slaves. They were generous and supported the church with their large gifts of personal leadership and financial resources.

Kinsey Burden, son of an Edisto planter of the same name, came to Johns Island in 1805 or 1806 and married Mary Legare, the sister of Thomas Legare Jr., daughter of the senior Thomas Legare and Elizabeth Basnett and aunt to Mrs. Elipha (Elizabeth Legare) White.[48] Burden drafted a map of the island about 1830 that shows Oakvale, Thomas Legare's estate, where the Burdens lived and farmed.[49] Burden was a legend in his own time for his hybridization of Sea Island cotton, which could be grown on the Sea Islands in what are today Charleston, Colleton and Beaufort Counties. The staple length of fancy Sea Island cotton was about two inches, considerably longer than mainland cotton, and its thread could be woven into very fine cloth. It had a limited market but brought a very high price. On Edisto, William Seabrook and John Townsend also developed the seed, and the three of them, according to Richard D. Porcher, were "the icons of the industry" because they could obtain the highest price for their product.[50] The development of the crop required increasing numbers of skilled slaves, whom the owners and overseers carefully trained and managed in assigned tasks for the production of the crop. Cotton became king after the Revolutionary War and reached its pinnacle of produced value in 1860.

The Burden, Legare and Wilson families were among the elite class of planters who made the Sea Islands of South Carolina the wealthiest part of the United States in the antebellum era. Other prominent families who were leaders in the Johns Island church included: Beckett, Fludd, Fripp, Hay, Hills, Holmes, Jenkins, Mathewes, Pritchard, Schaffer, Seabrook, Taylor, Townsend, Walpole, Wescoat and Whaley. Elipha White, invited into this society as minister and through his marriage, had many privileges and large prestige to support his life's work as pastor on Johns Island.

The growing strength of the Johns Island congregation and its new minister from New England attracted resources for the congregation to enlarge its meetinghouse. George Howe records:

James Legare (1762–1830) married Mary Wilkinson (1764–1841). James and his brother, Thomas Legare Jr. (1766–1842), were elders and important leaders during the ministry of Reverend Elipha White. Portrait by Samuel F.B. Morse (1791–1872). *Courtesy of the Walpole family.*

This was done by funds contributed for this purpose by members of the various denominations, Episcopal and Methodists, and Baptists, joining with heart and purse to assist these Presbyterians. The amount contributed from these sources was $3,645. The church came also into the possession of

A portrait of the children of James and Mary W. Legare by Robert Bogle. James Legare is on the left, Bryan Legare is standing (died young), the girl holding the baby is Lydia Bryan Legare and the baby is Mary Legare. *Courtesy of the Walpole family.*

about $4,000, from the old Johns Island Society, a charitable association, which had been in existence for some time, and employed its funds for various charitable purposes, among others for maintaining a seminary of learning, and relieving the indigent. It was incorporated December 9, 1799, and becoming nearly extinct, its funds were divided among the churches by the surviving members. By his deed of gift of July 6, 1820, Thomas Hunscombe [sic], who was not a member of any church conveyed to James Legare, Sen., Thomas Legare, Sen., and Hugh Wilson, Jun., Trustees of the Johns Island Presbyterian Church, fifty six-acres of land on the Island, and by his will gave and bequeathed to the Presbyterian Church of Johns Island, whatever may be its corporate name of title in law the sum of $6,000.[51]

The growing congregation required more room. The gifts from the other congregations, the Johns Island Society and Thomas Hanscome were large. The total comparable purchasing value in 2009 is approximately $293,000. However, if we consider the value of the gifts in the historical context, when natural resources were difficult to obtain and when slave labor would not have been compensated, the value of the gift would be worth considerably more.[52] The original footprint of the Georgian building was enlarged by twenty feet. The narrower seven-inch wainscoting of 1823 shows the line of the expansion in the Georgian original. Added galleries accommodated increasing numbers of slave members. They entered by the narrower end doors adjacent to the balcony, while white members entered by the side doors leading directly to the pews.[53] The architectural design reinforced the social distinctions of master and slave, even while uniting them together in common worship. The meetinghouse was enlarged and adapted for a new century of ministry. At the time, the members could have scarcely imagined the events ahead that would lead to the Civil War.

The gallery was added to the sanctuary in 1823, during the ministry of Reverend Elipha White. *Photograph by Katharine Bair.*

When White came, the practice of receiving slave members into the membership grew rapidly. This commitment was the first evangelical program that the congregation developed during his ministry. In the 1856 minutes of the session, the procedure, probably established during White's ministry, is described in the following record:

> *The following servants were received as members on examination, after having been two years under the care of the colored leaders, three months under the special instruction of the pastor of the Church, and after having brought tickets from their masters, certifying to their good moral character, and granting them permission to unite with the church.*

Upon acceptance by the session and baptism, the slave members attended worship and on Communion Sundays could come down from the balcony and stand at the table after the white members had been served.

The membership statistics reported by the Session to the General Assembly of the Presbyterian Church U.S.A. show remarkable growth in numbers during the first decade of Elipha White's ministry. The chart "Slave and White Members, 1825–1853" shows that from the year 1825 through 1833, the number of communicant members grew from 98 to 275. Most of these new members were by examination and baptism. In 1853, when the statistical report divided the numbers to indicate slave members ("colored"), the white communicant membership was twenty-nine adults, so the vast majority was slave members. In the first two decades of White's ministry, probably about two dozen were white communicants. Comparing the statistics in 1833 to those of 1853, four years after White died, shows a gain of over 300 percent, the vast majority of new members coming from slaves.

SLAVE AND WHITE MEMBERS, 1825–1853

YEAR	NUMBER OF COMMUNICANTS	ADULTS BAPTIZED	INFANTS BAPTIZED	ADDED ON EXAMINATION
1825	98	14	2	
1826	188	28	6	

Year	Number of Communicants	Adults Baptized	Infants Baptized	Added on Examination
1829	211	21	1	25
1830	230	26	11	27
1831	255	41		37
1832	295	34		31
1833	275	8		3
1853	359 (330 colored)	24		

The expansion of slave membership came about as a result of several important developments in the first decades of the nineteenth century. Coming out of the Second Great Awakening movement of missionary ministry, White enthusiastically embraced the evangelical commitment to preaching and teaching the gospel to every human being. He and his colleagues in the Presbyterian and Congregational churches shared this commitment with the other Protestant churches, including Episcopal and especially the Methodist and Baptist churches. The movement for instruction, baptism and receiving African American members into Congregational and Reformed Presbyterian churches received increasing emphasis.

Benjamin Palmer at the Congregational church in Charleston and Charles C. Jones, "the Apostle to the Negro Slaves," from Midway Congregational Church in Liberty County Georgia, wrote catechisms for the instruction of the slaves.[54] Jones's was widely used after it was published in the 1837. As part of its teaching, the catechism required that masters be kind and restrained in managing their slaves, and it taught that slaves were to be obedient to their masters. The instruction and inclusion of slaves in the worship of the community was both a sincere sharing of the ministry of Jesus Christ and, at the same time, a reinforcement of the foundations of social custom and economic reality. Charleston had seen a slave revolt planned by Denmark Vesey in 1822, soon after White arrived. The plot had been discovered and met with swift trial and punishment. People in the city feared an independent African American church. In the country, restriction on travel and communication hampered organized secret rebellions. Still, as the letter of Ichabod Brewster shows, Johns Island residents were fearful of revolt. The white lay and pastoral leaders of all the churches were convinced that it was good for the ordering of society, as well as the welfare of the slaves, to preach the gospel to the slave population, baptize and receive them into the church.[55]

Elipha White and other pastors in the Charleston area took very seriously their role in leading their congregations to take responsibility for the religious instruction of the slaves. However, the Johns Island and Wadmalaw Presbyterian Church excelled. It became the second largest Presbyterian congregation in the South in 1860.[56] That year, it reported 510 black members and 60 white members. This number was about three times as large as the Edisto Island Presbyterian Church membership and almost two and a half times as large as that of the James Island Presbyterian Church.[57] The fervor and consistency with which the Johns Island and Wadmalaw Church provided for the teaching, baptism, worship and instruction of slaves developed a very strong African American Presbyterian community. This lasting contribution of the congregation, undertaken while White was its pastor, led the slaves, after the war, to establish five African American Presbyterian congregations on Johns Island and Wadmalaw Island. The African American Presbyterian community continues to serve on Johns Island today.

Johns Island took a progressive lead in a second evangelical cause: foreign missions. In December 1836, White preached a sermon, "The Genius and Moral Achievements of the Spirit of Foreign Missions." It was published in a pamphlet in Boston in 1837 and was twenty-two pages in length. It must have taken three-quarters of an hour to deliver. The sermon shows White's gift of speaking in a careful outline and his repetition of themes and summaries in an eloquent style. The theology is broad, interdenominational in perspective, and it appeals to the progressive building of morality and civilization through the spirit of foreign missions. The spirit of missions is the spirit of Christ, who obeyed God and endured the sacrifice on the cross for man's redemption. The spirit of missions comes to us from the Bible, and it lives today among those who say, "Lo, I come to do thy will, O God" (Hebrews 10:9). The spirit of missions is "humble, peaceable, long-suffering, persevering, and overpowering."

Bringing the message home to his congregation, White emphasizes that "the recent efforts of Christian benevolence," the cooperative movement to

The Genius and Moral Achievements of the Spirit of Foreign Missions.

A

SERMON

PREACHED IN THE PRESBYTERIAN CHURCH,

JOHN'S ISLAND, S. C.

DECEMBER 18, 1836.

BY REV. ELIPHA WHITE,
PASTOR.

BOSTON:
PRINTED BY CROCKER & BREWSTER.
47 Washington Street.

1837.

A published sermon by Reverend Elipha White in support of the missionary work of John Leighton and Mary B. Wilson to Africa. *Courtesy of Presbyterian College.*

bring light and civilization to heathen lands, is the contemporary challenge. This moral task invites literature and scientific discovery. It raises the estimation of females "to the rank for which they were designed"—"equals, companions, friends." Foreign missions elevate the standard of morality and promotes the piety and happiness of mankind. White's sermon represented the evangelical theology of the interdenominational benevolent societies of the Second Great Awakening. It was written at the invitation of the Southern Board of Foreign Missions, and he dedicated it to the board. His theology is not the high Calvinism of the Westminster Confession, though White claimed that he embodied its spirit. Rather, he emphasized a ecumenical piety that would appeal to highly cultured listeners and their sense of moral conviction in support of an enlightened Christianity and culture.

The minister and officers of the church had carefully prepared for the mission's emphasis. At the semiannual meeting of the corporation, the congregation meeting after worship promised its support for John Leighton Wilson as a missionary to Cape Palmas in Africa. The church pledged to give $600 annually for five years. Today, this sum would be worth about $15,000 a year in consumer value; then, it was a good year's salary for a minister. The resolutions are signed by Thomas Legare, chairman of the corporation, and Kinsey Burden Jr., secretary. Wilson was one of the greatest missionaries in the Presbyterian Church. In 1854, he returned to the United States and became the secretary of the Board of Foreign Missions.[58] This action, at a time of the congregation's strength, provided an enduring model that has been continuingly reaffirmed throughout the history of the Johns Island Presbyterian Church. Support for world missions has been a notable focus of the congregation's attention since the ministry of Elipha White. It continues today.

A third benevolent commitment of the congregation was in the founding of the Theological Seminary at Columbia. The growing need for ministers in the South caused leaders in South Carolina to press for the establishment of a new seminary. Schools of divinity abroad and in the Northeast had supplied most of the ministers in South Carolina until the third decade of the century, but Andover, Princeton, Yale and Harvard could no longer fill the need. Furthermore, a growing sense of the particular requirements of the Georgia and South Carolina section of the country called for a local

John Leighton Wilson, missionary to Africa, sponsored by Johns Island Presbyterian Church. *C. Benton Kline Jr. Special Collections and Archives, John Bulow Campbell Library, Columbia Theological Seminary. Used by permission.*

The campus of the theological seminary in Columbia. In Charleston Union Presbytery, the Reverend Elipha White was in charge of raising funds for the establishment of the seminary in Columbia in 1829. *C. Benton Kline Jr. Special Collections and Archives, John Bulow Campbell Library, Columbia Theological Seminary. Used by permission.*

commitment to theological education.[59] In 1812, Union Theological Seminary was founded as the theological department of Hampden-Sidney College in Virginia, but its first professor was not appointed until 1822, and then its regional commitment was to provide ministers in Virginia and North Carolina. Both South Carolina and Georgia formed Education Societies, and the synod formed the Theological Seminary of South Carolina and Georgia in 1828. The presbyteries in the two states had twenty candidates for the ministry between them in 1829, when they decided to place the new institution in Columbia.[60]

White garnered support for pastoral training in the educational benevolence societies. Thomas Legare and William Seabrook of Edisto, along with other donors in and around Charleston, gave generous support to the new seminary. Aaron Leland, pastor of James Island and First

(Scots) Presbyterian Church, became professor in 1833. Elipha White was appointed as a member of the board of the theological seminary, was on the seminary's committee to revise the 1833 charter and became the agent for it within the bounds of Charleston Union Presbytery. From 1831 to 1837, he paid $5,072 into the seminary treasury. Today, the value of this gift is about $134,154, using the consumer price index as a measure.[61] White clearly had the confidence of his Presbyterian and Congregational colleagues and large numbers of lay people in the churches for leading the compelling campaign to build the Theological Seminary in Columbia.

The final notable event in the life of the Johns Island Presbyterian Church during Elipha White's ministry was its determination to become independent of all denominational ties. This action to separate came partly as a result of the Old School–New School division in the national Presbyterian denomination. Its roots also grew from the gathering political storm that, twenty-five years later, would lead to the secession of South Carolina from the United States of America.

In 1822, the Congregational Association of South Carolina united with Harmony Presbytery and then the Congregational and Presbyterian churches in the Charleston area to organize Charleston Union Presbytery.[62] Dr. Benjamin Palmer, pastor of the Circular Congregational Church, was the first moderator. Elipha White and Aaron Leland were among the founding pastors. During these years, the Presbyterian denomination was changing, and a debate was underway between an Old School and a New School. The Old School strength was from the Scots-Irish members, who for a century had been coming into the Presbyterian Church in the United States of America.

In the first decades of the nineteenth century, Old School leaders, who increasingly identified with Princeton and Columbia Theological Seminaries, were conservative in their views about the Westminster Confession and Presbyterian polity, with its strong governance by presbytery, synod and general assembly. The New School emphasized developments in New England Calvinism, especially from Congregational churches, including a looser interpretation of the Westminster Confession, an emphasis on local church governance, the development of independent benevolence societies for the promotion of education, evangelism and missions and the revivalism that grew out of the Second Great Awakening. In addition, the New

EDUCATION.

AN

INTRODUCTORY DISCOURSE,

BEFORE THE

AMERICAN INSTITUTE OF INSTRUCTION,

DELIVERED IN WORCESTER, MASS.

AUGUST 24, 1837.

BY REV. ELIPHA WHITE,

Of John's Island, S. C.

BOSTON.

PRINTED BY I. R. BUTTS,

No. 2, SCHOOL STREET.

1837.

A copy of the address by Reverend Elipha White to the American Education Society presented to Reverend Thomas Smyth, minister of Second Presbyterian Church, Charleston, South Carolina. *Courtesy of Presbyterian College.*

School was committed to the emancipation of the slaves. Some members were sympathetic to abolitionists who wanted immediate emancipation. Others on both sides of the debate about slavery hoped for the gradual development of conditions that would make emancipation possible. In 1837, the Presbyterian Church split between Old School and New School over all of these issues, and it remained divided until 1869 in the North. The southern Presbyterian Church, particularly through the influences of Princeton Theological Seminary, the Theological Seminary in Columbia and Union Theological Seminary in Richmond, was dominated by Old School commitments well into the twentieth century.[63]

The debate in the 1820s in South Carolina was not about theological considerations or church government so much as it was about how the church could and should respond to slavery. In 1818, the Presbyterian General Assembly had declared:

> *We consider the voluntary enslaving of one part of the human race by another, as a gross violation of the most precious and sacred rights of human nature; as utterly inconsistent with the law of God, which requires us to love our neighbor as ourselves; and as totally irreconcilable with the spirit and principles of the Gospel of Christ, which enjoin that "all things whatsoever ye would that men should do to you, do ye even so to them." Slavery creates a paradox in the moral system—it exhibits rational, accountable, and immortal beings, in such circumstances as scarcely to leave them the power of moral action.*[64]

This statement replied to a question from a local church about whether it was legitimate for a member to sell a slave who was also a member of the church. Beyond stating that slavery was contrary to the gospel, it urged the deliberate emancipation of slaves and endorsed the American Colonization Society's advocacy for returning freed slaves to a country of their own in Africa. Most prominent Presbyterian ministers in South Carolina supported the emancipation of slaves but felt that freedom must wait on the gradual progress of society. In addition, until South Carolina seceded and the Civil War began in 1861, they supported the Union. Leaders like John Witherspoon in Camden and Thomas Smyth at Second Presbyterian Church in Charleston favored a moderate stance between abolitionism's call for immediate emancipation and radical proslavery advocates.[65] The moderate voice prevailed at the General Assembly of 1836, which resolved, "It is not expedient for the Assembly to take any further order in relation to this subject."[66] The Synod of South Carolina and Georgia ruled that slavery is a "domestic institution…it is one on which no Judicatory of the Church has the right or power to legislate." The moderates advocated the silence of the governing bodies of the church on civil matters. This view was defended for the next quarter century in the most thorough way by James Henley Thornwell (1812–1862), the best-known teacher at the Theological Seminary in Columbia, and it became widely embraced in the southern Presbyterian Church.

Ministers—like Elipha White and William Dana at Third Presbyterian—who had been members of the Congregational Church even though on other grounds they were more in accord with New School Presbyterian ideas would have nothing to do with moderation on the topic of slavery. They agreed with most of their church members that slavery was necessary for their way of life and defensible on Christian grounds. Furthermore, because their roots were in the Congregational Church, they believed that in matters of faith and order, the vote of the congregation determined policy. The former Congregational pastors held the majority in Charleston Union Presbytery, and they elected White to attend both the 1837 and 1838 General Assembly meetings. He attended the latter with Thomas Smyth of Second Presbyterian Church, a moderate on the question of slavery. The majority of the presbytery instructed White to have the antislavery statement of 1818 repealed and to declare that a slaveholder had the right to preach the gospel. However, the 1838 General Assembly was preoccupied with the Old School–New School denominational division. White's memorial for Charleston Union Presbytery was tabled without discussion.

In the Synod of South Carolina and Georgia, advocacy of a separate Presbyterian denomination began to develop. I.S.K. Legare, brother-in-law of Elipha White and pastor at Orangeburg, led the charge, but the synod meeting of 1838 overwhelmingly defeated a proposal to establish a southern Presbyterian Church. The movement was more broadly supported in Charleston. In November 1838, three weeks after the synod met, Charleston Union Presbytery

Reverend James Henley Thornwell, professor at Columbia Theological Seminary, 1855–62. *C. Benton Kline Jr. Special Collections and Archives, John Bulow Campbell Library, Columbia Theological Seminary. Used by permission.*

voted against remaining in the Presbyterian Church. Thomas Smyth and five others remained with the denomination and formed a new Charleston Presbytery. Elipha White and Thomas Legare returned to Johns Island determined to make the Johns Island church an independent Presbyterian congregation.

Reverend Thomas Smyth, minister, Second Presbyterian Church, Charleston, South Carolina. *C. Benton Kline Jr. Special Collections and Archives, John Bulow Campbell Library, Columbia Theological Seminary. Used by permission.*

On December 24, 1838, the majority of the corporate members of the Presbyterian Church of Johns Island and Wadmalaw declared their independence from "all connection with the Charleston Union Presbytery, and every other ecclesiastical body, and placed upon the same ground occupied by other Presbyterian Churches in our neighborhood."[67] They were thinking of the independent Presbyterian churches of James Island, Edisto Island, Wilton and others incorporated by South Carolina in 1785.[68] White supported these resolutions but requested to be excused from voting. Twelve persons voted for the resolutions: Thomas Legare, Kinsey Burden Sr., John A. Fripp, William Beckett, Charles E. Fripp, Solomon Legare, James L. Walpole, Kinsey Burden Jr., Horace Walpole, J.C.W. Legare, D. Selyer and Mr. Laussey. Three persons voted against: Hugh Wilson Sr., John F. Townsend and Hugh Wilson Jr.

This secession from the presbytery and the Presbyterian Church on Christmas Eve could not have been a joyous occasion, even if those who won felt satisfied and right. They were determined to defend "Southern institutions," as they called it. They meant to have the Presbyterian Church revoke its declaration that slavery was a violation of the law of God and its commitment to emancipation, whether gradually or immediately. At the General Assembly, White's effort to repeal the 1818 resolution against slavery and the move at the Synod of South Carolina and Georgia to separate from the Presbyterian Church had failed. Back at home, the Independent Presbyterian Church of Johns Island and Wadmalaw congregation resolved, "With unabated attachment to the doctrines, discipline and order of the Presbyterian Church, we will sustain her standards as based up God's work, inviolate."

The matter did not end with this resolution. Hugh Wilson, William McCants, Edward Beckett and Hugh Wilson Jr. withdrew from the independent corporation, organized as a congregation under the jurisdiction of the General Assembly, elected officers and claimed to be the true Presbyterian Church of Johns Island and Wadmalaw. They requested that the independent corporation turn over all books, paper, accounts, funds or other property. The request was refused, and the minority brought civil suit in 1839. Wilson and the other members of the minority lost their claim in the first ruling and then appealed in 1842.[69] In February 1846, the court

Kinsey Burden Sr., whose gravestone is shown, was married to Mary Legare (1775–1852) and was an elder and important leader in the church during the ministry of Reverend Elipha White. *Photograph by Katharine Bair.*

recognized the South Carolina incorporation of the congregation and the role of the presbytery in governing the membership of ministers and authorizing the call of a Presbyterian congregation to a minister.[70]

On May 29, 1846, the corporation of the congregation met, rescinded the declaration of independence of December 24, 1838, and confirmed the authority of Charleston Union Presbytery over the Presbyterian Church of Johns Island and Wadmalaw. In 1852, the Old School General Assembly of the Presbyterian Church U.S.A. met in Charleston and cleared the way to receive Charleston Union Presbytery; the synod approved, and the remaining members of Charleston Union Presbytery merged with Charleston Presbytery.[71]

Elipha White and the lay leaders of the church carried it to a position of prominence. White was an extraordinary minister, with great personal gifts

Memorial to Reverend Elipha White, DD (1785–1849). *Photograph by Katharine Bair.*

and bearing. He was well known in both the North and South. He endeared himself to the people, including many African American members, who joined the Johns Island church in greater numbers than any other white congregation. He led them in early support for John Leighton Wilson, one of the greatest missionaries to Africa in the nineteenth century. He also supported and raised large sums for the establishment of the Theological Seminary in Columbia. On the question of slavery, he supported the status quo, and his strength of character, remembered in his epitaph as "inflexible firmness," led him to join with his elders and declare the church an independent congregation. He died in a fall from his horse at age fifty-four, three years after the congregation became reunited with the Presbyterian Church U.S.A. on November 20, 1849. For almost twenty-eight years, Johns Island and Wadmalaw had been his only pastorate.

JOHNS ISLAND AND WADMALAW PRESBYTERIAN CHURCH, 1850–1868

After the death of Elipha White, the congregation had an interim without a pastor of about four years. The Johns Island and Wadmalaw Presbyterian Church sent its first commissioner to Charleston Presbytery in 1853 and requested the installation of the Reverend A. Flinn Dickson as minister.[72] By 1855, the year of the earliest session minutes available, the session was meeting in good order. Elders from 1856 were Daniel Jenkins Townsend, MD, and John A. Fripp. Fripp remained clerk until he died on March 13, 1870, when John B.L. Walpole was elected as his replacement. Fripp and Walpole, two prominent leaders in the church and community, had both voted with the congregation to withdraw from the Presbyterian Church in 1838, but they remained in the congregation and served as members and officers, reconciled to the Presbyterian Church U.S.A. before the Civil War came. This unity was a credit to their charity and also the good ministry of A.F. Dickson. The congregation's leaders drew together and went forward united in connection with the Presbyterian Church.

During the ministries of Dickson and John R. Dow, who came in 1856, the nation was moving rapidly toward the crisis of the Civil War. South

Carolina ratified the constitution of the Confederate States of America on April 3, 1861, and nine days later, at 4:30 a.m., Charleston awakened to the bombardment of Fort Sumter. Abraham Lincoln was inaugurated in March, and Lincoln called for seventy-five thousand volunteers. In November, Port Royal fell, and Union ships patrolled the coast. General Robert E. Lee took command of South Carolina and Georgia. He considered the coast indefensible and abandoned all of the Sea Islands, except those necessary for the immediate defense of the harbor. On June 16, 1862, six thousand Union troops landed on James Island, but they were pushed back by five hundred Confederates at Secessionville.[73] This proud victory had no long-term defensive consequences, and in the summer of 1863, a siege of Charleston began. Morris Island was abandoned, and Fort Sumter was destroyed. Charleston held on in the midst of terrific destruction until it surrendered in February 1865 after siege and bombardment lasting 587 days.

John Reid Dow gave steady leadership as pastor through the great trauma of the Civil War, from 1855 to 1868, with a hiatus of four years during the war when the church dispersed. Dow was born in Scotland in 1811, came to the United States in 1839 and settled in Augusta as a merchant.[74] He married Catherine Carmichael in Augusta, where they became members of the First Presbyterian Church. In 1845, Dow became a candidate for the ministry and was licensed to preach by Hopewell Presbytery. On November 21, 1855, the Johns Island and Wadmalaw congregation elected him pastor, and the family moved on December 1, 1855.[75] On April 18, 1856, he came into Charleston Presbytery, which ordained and installed him as minister of the Johns Island and Wadmalaw Presbyterian Church. The record says:

> *The services are very solemn and impressive, and were performed in the presence of a large audience. Rev. Geo. Howe, D.D. of Columbia preached the sermon, presided and proposed the constitutional questions. Rev. John Douglas of James Island delivered the charge to the newly ordained Pastor, and Rev. W. States Lee of Edisto delivered the charge to the people. Rev. A.F. Dickson was present.*

With the "solemn and impressive" service, George Howe's distinguished leadership representing the theological seminary and the pastors from

Reverend George Howe, historian of the Presbyterian Church in South Carolina and professor at Columbia Theological Seminary, 1831–83, preached at the installation sermon for Reverend John Reid Dow in April 1856. *C. Benton Kline Jr. Special Collections and Archives, John Bulow Campbell Library, Columbia Theological Seminary. Used by permission.*

James and Edisto Islands, the unity and good hopes for the future of the congregation gave reason for gratitude to God.

From May 1856 to August 1861, the session met quarterly and on call to receive members. Daniel J. Townsend, MD, and John A. Fripp were

The Reverend John Reid Dow, minister, 1855–68. *Archives of Johns Island Presbyterian Church.*

regularly with the pastor; Kinsey Burden Sr. met occasionally. The session members decided in 1856 to add two elders and deacons, but it wasn't until 1859 that the congregation acted when it elected Hugh Wilson Sr. and W.S. Whaley, MD, as new elders. John B.L. Walpole, James J. Chisolm and Joseph L. Stevens were elected deacons.

The elders were attentive to receiving members. The session continued the practice of receiving African American members established during the ministry of Elipha White. For a slave to become a member required two years instruction under African American teachers, three months of instruction by the pastor and tickets from their masters certifying good moral character. This care and extensive training, combining the leadership of African American leaders and the pastor, made a lasting impression on hundreds of slaves on Johns and Wadmalaw Islands. They could not have all attended on any one Sunday, but the galleries could accommodate many. The session frequently exercised moral discipline, and quite a few African Americans were required to come before the elders for correction. A complaint, often brought by the masters, if substantiated resulted in suspension for varying lengths of time, according to the offense. The suspensions were subject to restoration after a specified time when the offending party brought evidence of genuine repentance.

After August 1861, life on Johns Island became more and more tenuous. Beginning in 1862, the islands south of Charleston were evacuated, and most residents sought refuge inland. The Mikell family from Edisto had a summer place in Aiken, and members of their family and their pastor, William States Lee, left the coast for the Aiken area.[76] Many from Johns Island took refuge in the upper part of the state. Reverend John Reid Dow, his wife and children went to Aiken.

Katherine Dow recorded her memory of the exile from Johns Island in the following notes, written years later in Aiken:

> *When Port Royal was bombarded the people on the island were afraid the enemy would soon come to the place, and they could not get away. Most of the families began to try to get off, first sending the women and children to safe places while the men remained to pack up what they could to try to save the crops and send their slaves and cattle into the "up country." The father of our UDC President, Mrs. Emanuel (the former Amelia Josephine Wilson of Ravenwood Plantation, Johns Island), was a member of Johns Island Church, and he was a good friend to the pastor, my father, and most kind to his family. The men of the church provided a boat and sent our family to Charleston, and there Father put his wife and five little girls on the train for Augusta, Georgia, where our aunts resided. Father and two little sons returned to Legareville, packed up the furniture and sent it to Augusta where it was stored in Clark's Mill, then called Carmichael Mill, which belonged to my mother's brothers.[77]*

Younger white males formed the Stono Scouts, with John Basnett Legare Walpole as captain. Later, they joined with the Third South Carolina Cavalry, led by Major John Jenkins of Edisto. Usually these units provided intelligence information for the defense of Charleston, but engagements took place at Haulover Cut and at Waterloo Plantation. In 1864, Captain Walpole and Major Jenkins had the summer village of Legareville burned to keep its material from the enemy.

After April 12, 1862, exactly one year following the bombardment of Fort Sumter, and until January 13, 1867, the church was closed, and the session called no meetings. The meetinghouse survived the war, and the congregation was able to continue after the war because of strong and devoted leadership by Dow and lay leaders, particularly Daniel Jenkins Townsend and John Fripp.

At last, after an interval of almost five years, the record notes the only reference to the Civil War in the minutes:

> *The church was dispersed by the late war, and for several years our sanctuary was closed. The Pastor Rev. John R. Dow was invited in the beginning of the year 1862 to supply the pulpit of the Presbyterian church at Aiken S.C. This invitation he accepted. At the earnest solicitation of the congregation he resumed his labours on Johns Island on 18 Nov. 1866. During the War the following members of the church died, and their bodies now lie in various parts of the state. Viz. Mr. Hugh Wilson, Se., Elder, Mr. J.J. Chisolm, Mrs. Geo. Rivers, Mrs. B. Mathews & Mrs. White.[78]*

This spare record does not reveal the anguish and disruption the people of the church felt during the war. In the word of the deaths of honored members, the names of Hugh Wilson Sr. and Mrs. White stand out. Wilson filed the suit for the restoration of the congregational property to the membership of the congregation after the split and declaration of independence of 1838. Mrs. White was the wife of the minister who led the church to declare its independence over the issue of slavery. They were united in the congregation, and their passing was noted with affection. The record gives notice of the passage of the Civil War and the turning of the generation toward the future.

During the final two years of Dow's service, five members joined or returned to reunite with the congregation. Miss Lydia M. Walpole and Miss Anna E. Dow transferred by certificate from Aiken. In 1867, Mrs. Joseph L. Stevens, John H. Townsend and Daniel Townsend became members. Joseph Stevens had been elected deacon in 1859.[79] He was appointed by the session to lead services when Dow was absent in November for the General Assembly meeting in Nashville. The session asked Dow to request funding at the General Assembly for the congregation:

It was resolved that our minister be requested to present the cause of our church during his absence, to the liberality of Christians and congregations, as Providence may open the way for him to do so. We need pecuniary aid to support the Ministry amongst us for the present, to repair the country church and the Manse, to build a church and a Manse at Legareville, and to erect several parochial schools. It is impossible for the people on these islands, in their present desolated and impoverished condition to do this, and it is hoped that the people of God at a distance may assist us in this great work, so much needed.[80]

The war changed Johns Island forever. Even with the return of residents after the war, the church and the community were "desolated and impoverished." The congregation had been a home mission field in the early years of the nineteenth century before the arrival of Elipha White; the Civil War left it a needy congregation, requesting denominational benevolences for its work of rebuilding.

In the hiatus caused by the Civil War, all of the African American members left the Johns Island congregation. During Reconstruction, many of them would become members of new African American churches. However, there is record of two African American married couples who requested membership and whom the session received: "The following colored persons appeared before Session and were examined as usual, and were received and communicants in our church. Viz. James Scott and his wife Masel Scott, Jacob Mitchell and his wife Betty Mitchell." These are the first African American members who joined at their own request after the war. They were received as any other married couples, not as servants under special instruction, and their first and last names were listed. Another "colored woman," Sarah Patterson, asked to be admitted on certificate. "Her letter was in order but it was thought advisable to postpone action in her case until next meeting."[81] The action was never taken. After the Scotts and the Mitchells, no other African Americans became members of the Johns Island Wadmalaw congregation.

Dow remained as minister for almost two years after he returned, until October 19, 1868, when he took the pastorate of the Salem Presbyterian Church, Black River, and Mrs. Dow and their daughters, Mary and Ann, were dismissed to that church. Later in the 1870s, Charleston Presbytery installed Dow as evangelist. He and Mrs. Dow returned to Aiken, where they remained for the rest of their lives. Mrs. Dow died in 1892. On December 23, 1895, after visiting friends, the eighty-four-year-old minister died, having begun at Johns Island forty years earlier.

RECONSTRUCTION AND RECOVERY, 1868–1898

Abraham Lincoln's Emancipation Proclamation took effect in January 1863, and many thousands of freedmen occupied their former masters' plantations. As General William Tecumseh Sherman marched from his victories in Georgia into South Carolina, many former slaves followed his army. Sherman issued Special War Order No. 15 to deal with the emergency caused by the refugees. The order set aside lands from Port Royal to Charleston and all abandoned rice fields along rivers to thirty miles inland for the benefit of the freed slaves.[82] The plantations were rented in small parcels for occupation and could be purchased at the end of three years. President Andrew Johnson set aside the Order No. 15 after about a year, at which time original owners could come back to claim their property.

The South Carolina Land Commission purchased tracts of land and resold them to small farmers. The Freedmen's Bureau, created to administer emergency food and relief after the war, worked to establish rightful ownership and oversee the mediation of contracts for labor and wages. In contrast to 1860, when only 359 farming units of large acreage stretched from Bull Island to Hilton Head, in 1870, the number of farms was 2, 261, and most of them were much smaller.[83] On Johns Island in 1860, there were 61 large farms and plantations; in 1870, there were 400, many of them small tracts. Approximately 300,000 acres changed hands. Half of the holdings were owned by African Americans, who bought land with money gleaned from their own labor.[84]

Members of Johns Island and Wadmalaw Church faced the economic disaster following the Civil War. Former plantation owners who could hold on and continue farming reduced their working acreage, hired laborers and worked to produce crops. Production and prices were down. For example,

Daniel Jenkins Townsend on Wadmalaw, whose slaves produced 140 bales of cotton at 400 pounds each in 1860, produced 8 150-pound bales in 1870.[85] Later, Francis Yonge Legare acquired large acreage at Mullet Hall and farmed it successfully with wage labor. Still later, Charles Andell, his brother and sister-in-law, William and Marguerite Andell, and Ferdinand Shaffer came from New York, purchased land on Johns and Wadmalaw Islands and set up successful farms. The people of the Presbyterian church held on and enabled the church to move forward. New pastors and members brought a new day of leadership to meet the hard times. The resilience of families and a new generation of residents fueled the long recovery leading through hard times to the twentieth century.

After Dow left in 1868, the next pastor, Reverend J.B. Mack, came in May 1869. People began coming to the island and joining the church. Horace Walpole and Miss Emma Beckett came from Zion Presbyterian Church in Charleston. The session examined Francis Y. Legare and received him as a member in June; he would become a very important lay officer in the coming years. Other leaders for the new generation were adding support. On June 12, 1870, the congregation met at the home of Dr. William S. Whaley in Legareville and elected John B.L. Walpole and Joseph L. Stevens as ruling elders. "This addition to the Eldership was rendered necessary by the death of Elder John A. Fripp, who fell asleep in Jesus on March 13, 1870."[86] In October, Captain Walpole was elected clerk of session, and he served until his death in 1894. Joseph Stevens soon attended the seminaries in Richmond, Virginia, and Columbia and returned later (1880) as pastor.

The session met only two more times during the time Reverend Mack served, and these were to elect delegates to the presbytery and synod. The congregation was struggling for leadership. The frequency of worship services during this time is unknown. Perhaps one of the officers gathered the congregation when no minister was available.

The Reverend Franklin Leonidus Leeper was called in April 1873 from status as an evangelist on the coast to the pastorates of the James Island and Johns Island and Wadmalaw Churches, where he remained until 1877.[87] Leeper was from Alabama and had served in the Confederate army. While he was a student at the Theological Seminary in Columbia from 1868 to 1871, he married Janie Crawford in 1870.

Reverend Franklin Leonidas Leeper, minister, 1873–77. *C. Benton Kline Jr. Special Collections and Archives, John Bulow Campbell Library, Columbia Theological Seminary. Used by permission.*

In 1876, the session presented for the first time an annual statistical report in a new form set by the denomination:

Number of Elders	*3*
Number of Deacons	*2*
Communicants added on examination	*6*
Communicants added on certificate	*2*
Total of Communicants	*30*
Adults baptized	
Infants baptized	*2*
Number of baptized non-communicants	*30*
Funds Collected	
Sustentation	*$12.16*
Evangelistic	*4.95*
Foreign Missions	*12.58*
Education	*28.96*
Presbyterial	*8.45*
Congregational	*25.51*
Pastor's Salary actually paid	*369.81*

Leeper also wrote a "Narrative of the State of Religion in the Johns Island and Wadmalaw Church."[88] The church, he reported, is a "limited field" yet in miniature, "a picture of the Church of Christ in all the earth...For several years we have had to mourn over our Spiritual coldness and the want of growth in our numbers." Some older members, he continued, have been

> *transferred from the Church Militant to the Church Triumphant...Our young men and maidens seemed to have been given over to worldliness, and more came forward to fill the places in our ranks where saints had fallen.* [Still,] *God remembered mercy and turned from us his anger and we are rejoicing in, what we believe are the first fruits of the harvest...* [Their reason for gratitude is] *in the faithfulness with which God has afflicted us...He hath in mercy spoiled our pleasant places and disappointed our earth-born hopes and prospects...Today we find manifest on the part of our people a spirit of more cheerful submission to God's will than has been since the close of the war.*

The Nineteenth Century

The language of the day was formal, with quotes of scripture and a style that seems overly submissive to our hearing today. Yet we can see that the report shows how the people felt in the days of Reconstruction on the island, eight years after the Civil War. The turn of phrase reflects the language of worship. It is penitential, recognizing the bitterness of their disappointment in the outcome and effects of the war. Its final note is gratitude. Particularly striking is the understanding that God caused their disappointment because their hearts were "so materially prone to evil." The session expressed thanksgiving for the increased attention the church and worship received and for the "manifest increase in love for the church." In the elegant penmanship of Captain Walpole, the clerk, these words record the heartfelt self-examination of the minister and elders on behalf of the people whom they felt God had called them to serve. Leeper left in 1879 to serve in Mount Pleasant and other churches in the Carolinas and Tennessee. He returned to James Island in 1893–94.

Meanwhile, many of the African American Presbyterians who had been members of Johns Island and Wadmalaw Presbyterian Church established their own churches. In cooperation with the Freedman's Bureau, missionaries from the Presbyterian Church U.S.A. came to the South to help with humanitarian assistance, to start churches and to build schools to educate former slaves and their children. Both black and white missionaries came to serve churches and teach. Often sanctuaries and schools were built together, and the pastors and wives served as teachers. By 1872, four churches had been established within a few miles of Johns Island and Wadmalaw Presbyterian Church: Bethel, Hebron, Zion and Salem on Wadmalaw.[89] Later, Buleau (St. Andrews) was built across the Stono River on the mainland.

The rationale for this home mission work in the South was stated in a report (1866) to the General Assembly of the Presbyterian Church in the United States of America by the assembly's Committee on Freedmen:

The Committee have done a good work. They have raised funds to the amount of $25,000—have fifty-five missionaries in commission, over three thousand pupils in their school, and over two thousand in Sabbath Schools. The condition of those whom they seek to benefit is one of depression and dependence, and, in many instances, of deep degradation. If they are not to *become a disturbing and dangerous element in society, they must be educated to take care of themselves. They must have the Bible, the school, and the gospel with all its purifying and elevating influences.*[90]

The African American churches were members of Catawba Presbytery, encompassing churches in North and South Carolina, until 1868, when Atlantic Presbytery was formed.[91] Catawba Presbytery met in Charleston in 1866 and received several pastors. The Reverend Ishmael Moultrie became pastor of the Edisto Island Presbyterian Church and served Salem and St. Andrews Churches on Wadmalaw and the mainland. The Reverend S. Campbell was pastor of the Johns Island Presbyterian Church, which later became Bethel, Hebron and Zion Churches. In 1873, the congregations combined reported 430 members. Even though by 1880 18 to 20 percent of the African Americans who had been members of white churches before the war left the Presbyterian denomination, on Johns Island a large African American Presbyterian membership remained loyal to the Presbyterian Church U.S.A.[92] Before the Civil War, they had been instructed and received into the Johns Island and Wadmalaw Presbyterian Church. After the war, they had their own pastors, who built churches and provided schools.

After F.L. Leeper left the Johns Island and Wadmalaw Church, Joseph L. Stevens came in 1880. Stevens had been ordained as an elder in 1870 and attended Union Theological Seminary in Virginia. Although it seems unusual for an elder and family member to return to his home church, the Johns Island congregation, like those of many other small Presbyterian churches, was dominated by strong families. In contemporary congregational studies, its size is called a family-size congregation.[93] The main effective leadership in a family-sized and dominated congregation is by the matriarchs and patriarchs among the lay members. They run the church. The minister's main role is not organizational leadership but the pastoral care, preaching and teaching of the congregation. Stevens, the son of a prominent family in the congregation, became its minister. In the twentieth century, this pattern of a son of the church becoming its minister would repeat in the call to Reverend Theodore Ashe Beckett, who had a tenure of twenty-two years (1923–45).

The meetings of the session while Stevens was pastor routinely only reported action on matters like funds, budget and electing delegates to the presbytery and synod. Usually, J.B.L. Walpole attended the meetings of the church judicatories. The elders reviewed discipline of two members because of long absence from public worship and "other irregularities." In these cases, the pastor was asked to write or visit them and ask them to meet with the session for inquiry. In one case, a member was suspended. The session's intention was to restore members and reconciling problems that would have been disruptive in the small community. Daniel Jenkins, an elder who had frequently been absent, came to the session at his own initiative and explained his absence, and the session accepted his renewal of communion with the congregation, in accord with the purpose of the session's oversight in discipline.[94] The pastor became ill in 1883, and the session approved his vacation, to be extended "until his health be restored or he may return to his charge." The next meeting was in November, and since normally a fall meeting would have taken place in September or early October, the recovery might have been a long one.

Several additions to the membership during Stevens's pastorate brought strength to the church. Mr. and Mrs. Swinton Townsend joined in 1880 and Mr. John H. Wilson in 1881. Of particular importance for the renewal of the congregation was the Beckett family. In 1882, Mr. and Mrs. Theodore Ashe Beckett Jr. came by transfer of their letter from Andrews Memorial Church in the Presbytery of St. Johns, Florida, and in 1884, Mr. and Mrs. T.A. Beckett Sr., by letter of transfer from the Edisto Island Presbyterian Church. Dr. and Mrs. William S. Whaley and his daughters moved to Athens, Georgia, in 1885. Dr. Whaley had been a ruling elder since February 1859. To take Dr. Whaley's place, the congregation elected Francis Yonge Legare to the session on November 25, 1883. He would serve with great devotion as elder and, later, as clerk of session until October 7, 1905. John L. Stevens resigned on December 28, 1885, and moved to Georgia.

William Gildersleeve Vardell was called to serve the congregation on March 8, 1885. Vardell was born in Charleston on February 2, 1829. He married Jane Dickson Bell of Charleston on May 20, 1857. He served with Dr. John L. Girardeau as a member of the officers' staff in the Twenty-third South Carolina Infantry Regiment, Confederate States Army. The regiment saw action in Northern Virginia and Petersburg and in the coastal defenses of Charleston. Dr. Girardeau was chaplain to the regiment. Vardell was a ruling elder and lay preacher; he studied theology privately and was ordained on May 10, 1885, for service in the Johns Island church.

The congregation met on March 8, 1885, after the worship service to elect a pastor. Elder J.B.L. Walpole was moderator, since no pastor was available. The call read as follows:

> *The church of Johns and Wadmalaw Islands, being on sufficient grounds, well satisfied of the ministerial qualification of you, Licentiate W.G. Vardell and having good hopes from our past experience (or knowledge) of your labors, that your ministrations in the gospel will be profitable to our spiritual interests, do earnestly call you to undertake the pastoral office in said congregation, promising you, in the discharge of your duty all proper support, encouragement, and obedience in the Lord. And that you may be free from worldly cares and avocations, we do hereby promise and oblige ourselves to pay you the sum of two hundred ($200.00), for one half of your time, in singular half-yearly payments during the time of your being and continuing regular Pastor of this church.[95]*

The members of the calling committee, Francis Y. Legare, T.A. Beckett Jr. and J.B.L. Walpole, signed the call. The presbytery appointed well-known commissioners to install: Dr. John Lafayette Girardeau, Reverend James Bulloch Dunwoody and the former Johns Island Wadmalaw pastor, Reverend John Reid Dow. Dow was serving as an evangelist for Charleston Presbytery, living in Aiken. Dr. Girardeau, who was a native of James Island, had served the other two churches in the call to Vardell—New Wappetaw (1848) and Wilton (1850–1853)—and was pastor of Zion Church in Charleston from 1853 to 1861, during which time he preached to thousands of African Americans. He was beloved by many in the Lowcountry, including slaves and freemen. He became professor at the Theological Seminary in Columbia in 1875. Dunwoody was pastor in Walterboro at the time of the call to Vardell.

Considering Vardell's service as major in the army of the Confederate States, it was a gentle irony that the moderator of Charleston Presbytery, William Howell Taylor—born in New York City, educated at Yale and Princeton and who had served as chaplain in the U.S. Army in 1865—attested the ordination and installation of the new pastor of the Johns Island and Wadmalaw

Reverend John L. Girardeau was chaplain in the Twenty-third South Carolina Regiment, CSA, and preached at the installation of Reverend W.G. Vardell. *C. Benton Kline Jr. Special Collections and Archives, John Bulow Campbell Library, Columbia Theological Seminary. Used by permission.*

Presbyterian Church. Taylor was pastor at Aiken. Even while Captain Walpole, Girardeau and Vardell shared memories of military service, the twenty years following the war had brought an end to Reconstruction and possibilities for new communion and collegiality in the southern Presbyterian Church.

Vardell became an effective pastor during a term of more than twelve years. His effectiveness is a tribute both to his good leadership and the trust and confidence of the church's members. Captain Walpole and Francis Legare, who with Vardell made up the session, represented prominent families. They trusted Vardell, and the session minutes show their respect for him as minister, as well as deep personal affection for him. Their cooperative leadership as pastor and officers strengthened the congregation in a difficult time of poverty and the need to make a new way of life on the island.

The results were impressive. The congregation doubled in size during Vardell's pastorate. He encouraged and led a strong Sabbath school through his popular teaching of adults, development of teachers and officers for the youth and children and regular Sunday afternoon services and classes in Legareville and Rockville. He was an advocate for increased leadership by the Women of the Church and encouraged their organized work in the congregation and the larger community. He presided over the passing of the antebellum generation into the next one that would provide leaders for the beginning of the twentieth century. He led his elders to participate in Charleston Presbytery and the Synod of South Carolina, thus confirming that the congregation would move beyond its earlier congregational independence.

The continuing and most forbidding challenge to the congregation during Vardell's ministry was a financial one. Many people on the islands, including church members, were poor. Even the more well-to-do families, represented by Dr. Hugh Wilson, Dr. Whaley, J.B.L. Walpole, F.Y. Legare and E.M. Seabrook, were required to develop an entirely new way of making a living. Agriculture, based on wage labor, was difficult and uncertain for both farmers and laborers. The congregation as an organization had very limited cash resources and struggled to pay the $200 half-time annual salary to Vardell. In March 1886, the session received a resolution from the corporation of the church, signed by T.A. Beckett, secretary:

*Resolved, that in view of the stringency of the times the Session of the
church be requested to aid us towards the payment of the Pastors salary to
the extent of their ability, out of funds on hand, and that the Secretary be
authorized to make application for the same.*

F.Y. Legare took the records to Charleston Presbytery with the letter
explaining the stringency of the times.[96] By May, the congregation had
raised the meager portion of the salary, but the problem of payments
recurred, and two years later, the session joined with the New Wappetaw
congregation near McLellanville, where Vardell also served as pastor, in a
request to Charleston Presbytery for a contribution for their pastor's salary.
F.Y. Legare reported after the presbytery met that, "for prudential reasons,"
the committee did not present the resolution because they had reason to
believe it would be denied. Instead, the Johns Island congregation asked
the presbytery to make good on a grant of $200 approved two years before
but never paid. The presbytery also had very limited funds but agreed and
stipulated that the amount be paid to the salary of the minister for the three
churches where Vardell served part time: Johns Island, New Wappetaw and
Wilton near Adams Run.[97] Later, the Domestic Missions Committee aided
the congregation with $100, but in the depression in 1895 it gave notice that
the subsidy was no longer available. Because of financial limitations and
Vardell's declining health, the pastoral call was amended to half time with
the James Island Presbyterian Church. At the end of his ministry, when the
session granted its minister long medical leaves, Vardell remitted the back
salary owed during his absence.[98] The congregation struggled to pay the
salary throughout his thirteen years of service.

In spite of the hard times, the session approved regular payments to the
benevolence programs of the Presbyterian denomination through Charleston
Presbytery. It also gave assistance to poor members of the congregation. The
records note the contributions to Presbyterian Church causes. For example,
on October 1, 1885, at the quarterly meeting after the summer break, the
session discussed the distribution of the collections for benevolence causes,
and it remitted five dollars each to foreign missions, the Invalid Fund and
the Evangelistic Fund. Then, in December of the same year, it added five
dollars each to foreign missions and sustentation and "three dollars to Mr.

Stillman as a contribution to paying back salary due Rev. Jr. R. Dow."
Poverty overwhelmed some members, and the session, throughout Vardell's
ministry, made contributions to "a poor member," "needy persons" and
"widows" in the congregation and local community. For example, on April
11, 1886, Communion Sunday, the session reported, "The funds collected
this morning were donated to one of our needy members."[99] In subsequent
quarterly meetings, the session remitted its benevolence and, from the
morning collections, assisted "the needy of our congregation."[100]

The session faithfully sent commissioners to the Charleston Presbytery
and the Synod of South Carolina. For example, Elder F.Y. Legare reported
that he was faithful in attending all of the sessions of the presbytery meeting
in Summerville on October 8, 1889. He said, "It is a matter of great
gratitude to God to report that this meeting was free from unchristian and
unhappy discussions." He reported the work of two evangelists within the
bounds, one of whom was very successful, and the delegates contributed to
the building of a new church. The other "was not so and in general we were
not making a full use of the opportunities." He was glad to report that a
week of services conducted in New Wappetaw Church, where "our beloved
and faithful pastor has labored for the past few years, and now rewarded
in his labor by permitting him to see twenty-one souls added to the Fold
during one week of earnest devoted work, in which he was assisted by Dr.
Gerideau [sic], so well known and beloved by us all." He also "attended the
meeting of Synod at the town of Spartanburg Oct 25th"and was present at
as many of its sessions during its meetings as was in his power to attend. He
reported, "Able addresses were delivered on foreign & domestic Missions also
on Education and one of our Presbyteries (Harmony) was divided forming
the new Presbytery of Pee-Dee the old name (Harmony) being retained by
the other." Again, the meeting was free from dissensions, and he asked the
pastor to give thanks to God for the answer to the prayers of his people that
God has "restrained human passions and thus mercifully presided over the
meetings of the courts of His Church."[101]

After the spring meetings of the Charleston Presbytery, when the
churches brought their minutes for annual approval, the churches gave
narrative reports. Elder J.B.L. Walpole wrote a number of the narratives.
The reports are usually boilerplate, conforming literally to the required

answers. Sometimes, however, they reveal the mood of the congregation. At the session meeting on March 23, 1890, after receiving Mr. Whitemarsh S. Glover as a member, the narrative for the church year ending April 1, 1890 was read:

> *The pastor is able to say that the Elders by the grace of God are kept faithful in their endeavors to discharge their duties. He also testifies to the comfort and support he realizes in their sympathy and zeal. The attendance upon the Service of the Sanctuary is good and steadily increasing. The attention to the preaching of the Word is close and reverent and not without practical results. We have not been blessed of God with any special outpourings of the "Holy Ghost" yet we are not without tokens of His merciful presence with us, in that the children of the covenant come one by one and we rejoice with gratitude of this. Our members with few exceptions are careful in their deportment and of these we are thankful to say, some are giving evidence of decided amendments. The members are all interested in the Sabbath School and those to teaching are (excepting a few) members of the Bible Class. Family worship generally observed. The Sabbath is respected. The members are faithful in worshipping God with their substance and considering the embarrassments and difficulties under which they labor, are doing as well as could be hoped for, still the desire to do still better is upon them if it should please God to prosper them in their labors. Intemperance does not prevail, neither do these people participate in, or countenance worldly amusements. We do not undertake any work among the colored people. We still continue our afternoon services at Riverside and Rockville. The attendance upon these services is good and the effort is appreciated by the people. The pastor's salary is paid up. The ladies of our church are zealous co-workers and amidst pressing cares and duties, so well their part. We gratefully acknowledge God's goodness to us in the excellent spirit pervading our people and pray God may graciously continue this manifestation to us.*[102]

Vardell encouraged the development of women's societies, which were the foundation of the coming Woman's Auxiliary, founded in 1920 at Johns Island and Wadmalaw. The earliest women's organization was the Ladies

Working Society, begun in 1887. Mrs. J.E. Fripp, widow of the former clerk of session, was president, and Mrs. F.Y. Legare was treasurer. In 1890, when Mrs. Fripp died, Mrs. Legare was president. "They sewed, and sold to Negroes, chiefly. Their work has been to repair the Church, furnish it, keep and fence grounds and cemetery, mark all unmarked graves with marble head and foot stones, and to raise two memorial tablets."[103] They contributed to home and foreign missions and to the pastor's salary. When Reverend H.M. Parker came in 1890, the Ladies Aid Society was founded. Mrs. J.B.L. Walpole was its first president, and its primary emphasis at first was the monthly support of the pastor's salary.

Mrs. F.Y. Legare wrote some autobiographical reflections for a history of Presbyterian women. Her record gives us insight about a prominent church leader. Before marriage, she was Kate Seymour Walpole. Born in Charleston during the Civil War, she went to South Mulberry, the plantation of Dr. Sanford Barker on the Cooper River. She recalled:

Had a special little closet, I used to go in and pray when the Yankees were coming, in which I ever felt safe. Moved to Mobile, Ala., directly after the war. When fourteen years old, I worshipped for the first time in the Johns Island Church, the church of my fathers, riding about four or five miles in a cart behind a wagon, carrying the little organ belonging to Mrs. J.B.L. Walpole in order to have music, and my whole heart went out to it in its hardships and the noble efforts made by Capt. Walpole and his wife, who played for service, the organ came back for sacred music at home at night. My heart went out to the old church in love and loyal allegiance that has ever been a part of my life, my very soul and heart-life. These Sundays at the old church and efforts made to have things smooth, made a lasting impression. It was lovely in after years to go there a bride, and take up work for the Master with my honored husband who was then a deacon and gladly did I give my life work to it. After Mrs. Fripp's death I was made president (had always been treasurer for convenience) of Working Society, which ever did good work. After Miss Lily Carrere's removal to Mississippi was made president of Children's Missionary Society. Was always a teacher in Sunday School, and in every way helped and worked as God gave me opportunity gladly, loving the privilege, with heart and hand

> *and purse. Going ever with my husband to Presbytery when his health got*
> *bad, gave me an insight into the workings of the church events and general*
> *committees and was of great value to me and helped much the old church*
> *after his death, as there was but one elder in the session and he had never*
> *attended Presbytery up to that time, and with the knowledge gained I could*
> *"help him very materially and did,"—his words.*[104]

This reminiscence reflects events from her childhood during the Civil War until after her husband died in 1905. Her impressions tell us of her admiration for Captain and Mrs. Walpole, her deep appreciation for the church and her support for her husband's service as an elder in the congregation and in the presbytery and synod. She also reveals that, in a day when women were confined to public roles subordinate to men, she learned about the organization and work of the denomination and used her experience for her own contributions in the congregation through the women's societies. The women initiated care for the church building and the cemetery, and they made a regular contribution to the salary of the minister. This leadership helped the church "very materially."

During the last six years of Vardell's thirteen-year ministry, he dealt with serious illness. The elders, J.B.L. Walpole and F.Y. Legare, were very gracious, concerned for both the congregation and the pastor's well-being. In July 1891, Walpole noted that the pastor was granted vacation until September 1. It might have been as late as November before he was able to return, at which time the session gave thanks for his return and resolved:

> *We gratefully acknowledge this gift of His mercy; and we do lift our hearts*
> *in grateful acknowledgement for this, and all other mercies vouched safe*
> *to us, and humbly pray that he be spared to us during a long life, and be*
> *abundantly blessed in his labors.*[105]

Vardell was sixty-two years old at the time, five years younger than Walpole and twenty-one years younger than Legare. The two old veterans, Vardell and Walpole, had a special bond and great respect for each other. In the spring of 1892, the session explained Vardell's illness to the Charleston Presbytery and, on behalf of the congregation, asked permission to amend the pastoral call to three-quarters time—three Sundays out of the month at a salary of $500 annually. For the previous seven years, he had been serving the Wilton Church and the New Wappetaw Church, traveling each weekend quite a distance in different directions on alternate Sundays. Spared of the travel, the pastor could stay on the island. The church would get one more Sunday's preaching a month, and Vardell could slow down. He gave up leading the Sabbath school on Sunday mornings and the Sunday afternoon missions to Rockville and Legareville, where he had led afternoon worship and Bible studies.

Then another crisis came when J.B.L. Walpole died on October 13, 1893. F.Y. Legare, the lone elder acting as clerk, noted in February 1894, "Owing to the serious illness of our beloved pastor Rev. W.G. Vardell, and lamented death of our Senior Elder, J.B.L. Walpole, the regular quarterly meetings of the Session have not been held." Legare took charge of arranging for supply ministers, noting in September that services were held "as frequently during the last six months as circumstances would permit." The year 1893 also brought the great hurricane, and the Rockville church was severely damaged. Legare must have felt that the great storm, the untimely death of J.B.L. Walpole and the unwelcome absence of the pastor added up to a great trial for the only elder left, but he made the best out of the suffering of the people, providing devoted leadership that held the church together.

During his illness, Vardell lived in the home of his son, also a pastor, in New Bern, North Carolina. He returned for partial service after an absence of well over a year. Vardell's next session meeting was in April 1895. He wrote a personal note of appreciation to F.Y. Legare in the minutes:

> *The Pastor realizes that it is his duty to put upon record, the commendable diligence of Ruling Elder F.Y. Legare who has whilst contending with peculiar embarrassment, conducted services in the church, procured preaching & otherwise faithfully discharged his official duties during the Pastor's sickness.* [Signed] *W.G. Vardell, Pastor.*[106]

It must have been clear that Vardell would never be able to return to full service. However, the presbytery approved another amendment, and in May

Gravestones for Lydia B. Walpole and J.B.L. Walpole. *Photograph by Katharine Bair.*

1895, Vardell began leading services two Sundays a month on Johns Island and two at James Island Presbyterian Church. On fifth Sundays, Vardell preached at Rockville. In the summer of 1897, he took a six-week vacation. In November, Legare, the lone elder and clerk, recorded:

> *Our Pastor's physical condition was such as to necessitate his rest for a time, and visiting certain Mineral Springs for his health, he was accorded so long a vacation as he may desire, and he was earnestly and affectionately urged to remain at the Springs, or such place as his physician may deem necessary, till he feel restored and able to resume his place among us, from which we will miss him so much. There being no further business, Session adjourned, after prayer by the Moderator. Francis Y. Legare, Clerk.*[107]

When the pastor died in 1897, Legare wrote:

> *Whereas our Heavenly Father has in His inscrutable wisdom, seen fit to remove from us our beloved pastor, the Rev. W.G. Vardell, Resolved 1ˢᵗ*

SACRED TO THE MEMORY OF
OUR BELOVED PASTOR
REV. W. G. VARDELL
WHO ENTERED INTO REST DEC. 24, 1897.

ORDAINED TO THE OFFICE OF
THE SACRED MINISTRY IN THIS CHURCH
AND INSTALLED PASTOR MAY 1885.
DURING HIS ENTIRE MINISTRY HE POINTED OUT
TO US WITH CONSECRATED FIDELITY
AND A ZEAL BORN OF THE HOLY SPIRIT,
THE STRAIGHT AND NARROW WAY LEADING UNTO
ETERNAL LIFE, EMULATING IN HIS LIFE
THE DOCTRINES HE TAUGHT.
WE BELIEVE GOD NEVER TOOK A MORE
SPIRITUALLY MINDED MAN FROM EARTH TO HEAVEN.
THE SWEET, SPIRITUAL COMMUNION OF SUCH AN ONE
LEAVES A VACANCY THAT TIME CAN NEVER FILL.
IN ANSWER TO HIS PRAYERS, DOUBTLESS MANY BLESSINGS
HAVE BEEN SENT US AND WE THANK OUR HEAVENLY
FATHER FOR THE BLESSED PRIVELEGE OF HAVING
HAD THIS EARNEST, DEVOTED, FAITHFUL, ZEALOUS MAN
OF GOD IN OUR MIDST, TO TEACH US HIS WILL.

Memorial to Reverend W.G. Vardell (1829–1897). *Photograph by Katharine Bair.*

That this church has sustained an irreparable loss in the translation of this zealous, faithful, consecrated Minister of the Word, and that we wish to put on record our testimony, as to his untiring zeal, unselfish devotion, and great efficiency in the Master's service, throughout a pastorate covering more than twelve years. During this entire period his earnest scriptural preaching wise counsel and Godly example have been blessed to every man, not only in this church but in the whole community.

This tribute expresses the sincere gratitude of the congregation. Two decades before, the people of Johns Island had confronted the destruction left by defeat in the Civil War, including the end of the plantation economy, the burning of Legareville, the flight of the residents to other parts and the closing of the churches. During Vardell's ministry, the church gained strength and resources. It provided anchor to people returning to their homes and rebuilding.

Part III

THE TWENTIETH CENTURY

We can find four major periods in the story of Johns Island Presbyterian Church during the twentieth century: 1) the first quarter century, when the congregation was known as Johns Island and Wadmalaw Presbyterian Church; 2) the second period of about two decades, from 1924 to 1945, when Theodore Ashe Beckett was the pastor and the congregation took the name Johns Island Presbyterian Church; 3) the middle of the twentieth century, including the post–World War II period until 1972; and 4) the final quarter century, when the congregation entered a time of sustained growth and gained the momentum in membership, resources, worship and service that continues today.

As we think about these main periods, a good approach might be to ask, "What were the ministers, officers and members at large experiencing on Johns Island and in the life of the church?" The congregation grew as the twentieth century passed, and the transitions in its life brought new demands and new opportunities for its ministry. One way of understanding the development of a church is to pay attention to the number of members active in worship and the stewardship of resources the church gathers and uses for its ministry in the name of Jesus Christ. Studies suggest that when a church moves from a very small one, led primarily by strong families, to a congregation of 50 to 150 members, a healthy congregation will want a full-time minister and will expect a different kind of leadership from officers and minister.[108] This shift from small church to a congregation with its own pastor occurred during the second period, while Beckett was minister.

Another qualitative change in church life comes when the number of active members in the congregation rises above 150 and lasts until it reaches about 350 members. This congregation will require more staff members than a pastor alone, and the officers and members will need more programs than worship, Sunday school and pastoral care led by their minister. The Johns Island congregation reached this stage of growth during the ministry of Austin Clark Wiser in the period after 1972. Moreover, during the fourth period of the twentieth century, responding with care and planning to the rapid development in the population and economy of the coastal area, the congregation reached another landmark. It grew rapidly beyond 350 active members during the pastorates of Ray Davies and Ernest Gray to about 500 members at the end of 2002.

The effect of the spurts in growth in a congregation depends not only on the numbers but also on the outlook and spirit of the church's members, especially its officers. All congregations, like all human beings, feel stresses and strains in times of major change. However, a healthy congregation, like a healthy human being, with faithful attention to the Christian life of worship, prayer and discipleship—the main business of the church—can recognize its needs and live into a new and stronger day. In the last quarter of the twentieth century, the Johns Island congregation grew rapidly in active membership, financial resources and programs of ministry for the congregation, the community outside and the world beyond. In a time when the Presbyterian Church U.S.A. and other mainline Protestant denominations were losing members, the Presbyterian congregation on Johns Island was growing rapidly in response to a boom in population on Kiawah and Seabrook Islands and the increasing service economy that supported it. The remarkable development of the congregation, remembering its past while becoming open to new life, is the story of Johns Island Presbyterian Church in the twentieth century.

The first quarter of the century challenged the congregation. South Carolina was a poor state and within it the rural coastal areas were the poorest section.[109] At the end of the nineteenth century, the congregations on Johns Island and Wadmalaw Island struggled to find enough money to pay their part of the pastor's salary, shared with James Island Presbyterian Church, and to hold worship and church school classes on the Sundays when no preacher came. Yet the congregations maintained a stability that brought their members together in worship and work. Things on Johns Island remained pretty much the same for the first quarter of century, and so the stability in membership, resources and program was itself a tribute to the steady work of the people of the church, its elders and deacons and an active women's organization. Its ministers during this period offered capable leadership. They were Henry Middleton Parker, Paul Stanley McChesney and Milton Randolph Kirkpatrick.

The second period, during the two-decade pastorate of Theodore Ashe Beckett (1924–45), brought the congregation through the era of the Great Depression and World War II and to the beginning of a period of stronger ministry. Beckett provided faithful and effective leadership as the pastor to the church family into which he was born on Johns Island. He served the Presbyterian churches on Johns and Wadmalaw Islands, as well as the James Island Presbyterian Church. Taking the name Johns Island Presbyterian Church in 1924, even though it continued to share its minister, the congregation was asserting its wish to become independent, and it made progress toward becoming self-sustaining while Beckett was minister.

In the third major period, twenty-five years from 1947 to 1972, the congregation called five pastors: William Bartlett Gaston, Gaston Boyle, John Rodman Williams, Robert Wilbur Cousar and Fielding Dillard Russell. During these middle years, Johns Island began to change rapidly. This quarter century brought the turmoil of world and national events to Johns Island. The records of the officers and Women of the Church reflect, sometimes between the lines, tensions and new issues of the Cold War, the movement of civil rights, the first steps of humankind on the surface of the moon, the Korean and Vietnam Wars and the expanded role of women's leadership in church and society. The challenges also brought new opportunities. During this period, the congregation and its officers rallied behind strong pastoral work, remained loyal to the Presbyterian Church U.S.A. and strengthened the ministry and witness of the congregation. When we consider the fast pace and disorientation of these world and national events, the church can be very grateful that faithful lay and pastor leaders developed strong programs and good resources for the Presbyterians on Johns Island during this time.

The proof of their strength is evident in the fourth period, a new era in the final quarter of the century from the mid-1970s into the beginning of the twenty-first century. The church called Austin Clark Wiser, Ray Willis Davies and Ernest E. Gray as pastors. As Kiawah and Seabrook Islands flourished as resort and retirement communities, and as the city limits of Charleston spread to include parts of Johns Island, the growth in population and development of a service economy brought greater challenges and opportunities to community and churches on the islands. By the end of Gray's eleven-year pastorate in 2002, the congregation had developed very substantial resources, multiple staff leaders and a rich diversity of life and ministry. With the congregation's call to the Reverend Jonathan Van Deventer in 2003, the Johns Island Presbyterian Church was still working out its ministry in this new twenty-first century setting, making plans for the coming years. The sections in this part consider these four twentieth-century periods and document the church's path forward into the twenty-first century.

THE FIRST QUARTER OF THE TWENTIETH CENTURY

The congregation met on March 27, 1898, and elected the Reverend Henry Middleton Parker. A commission of the Charleston Presbytery installed him as pastor on July 10. Reverend George A. Blackburn from Arsenal Hill Presbyterian Church in Columbia preached the sermon, and Reverend H.R. Murchison, pastor at Edisto Island, gave the charge to the people. F.Y. Legare, clerk of session, reported that "the day being a very rainy one, the attendance [at] the installation service was very small, very much to the regret of very many of the community, who very much desired to attend. The services were very impressive and instructive and enjoyed by all."[110]

Parker was born in Charleston in 1854.[111] His father, Henry Middleton Parker Jr., was a missionary in China and was killed in 1861 in an insurrection. His mother, Marianna Rhett, took her son to Europe during the Civil War, and he was educated in Paris, Brussels and England.[112] He graduated from the Episcopal Seminary in Alexandria, Virginia, in 1877 and served in Liberia as a lay missionary. He was licensed and ordained as a Presbyterian minister in Mecklenburg Presbytery and served in Black Mountain, North Carolina, from 1893 until he was called to serve the Johns Island and James Island Presbyterian Churches, where he remained until 1906. Later, he was pastor in Georgetown, South Carolina, and Statesville, North Carolina, where he also served as professor and dean at Mitchell College, a Presbyterian woman's college.

The congregation responded well to the new pastor. He cultivated new leadership. At the initiative of the session, the congregation elected two new deacons; Frank L. Seabrook and H.C. Mühler were ordained and installed to office on January 22, 1899. The deacons organized for the repairs of the buildings. The great hurricane of 1893 had damaged the Rockville sanctuary and required extra resources. F.Y. Legare wrote:

> *While the disasters of the past year have made our contributions to the various beneficial causes less than we expected or hoped, yet compared with the previous year they have not fallen behind in the total and we are striving to establish the tenth of our increase as the minimum standard of our daily giving.*[113]

Mühler, a newcomer to the island, became a member of the congregation in 1896 from the Lutheran Church, and he brought the welcome gifts of a capable leader. He was elected elder in 1904 and led the congregation in an effective way through the passing of the older generation. He became clerk of session when F.Y. Legare died in 1905. Legare's faithful work as an officer extended forty-six years. He was born on June 11, 1850; professed faith in Christ on June 13, 1869; was ordained deacon on December 26, 1875, and elder on February 10, 1884; and served as clerk from 1894 until his death. He was a member of the congregation through five pastors.

Mühler wrote an appreciative tribute:

> *The Session of the Johns Island and Wadmalaw church would place upon record their deep sorrow for the death of Mr. F.Y. Legaré, their Senior Elder, and would express their high regard of his Christian character and their*

The gravestone for F.Y. Legare, clerk of session. *Photograph by Katharine Bair.*

profound sense of their loss through his removal as that of a most faithful and devoted Servant of God.[114]

Parker encouraged the people to establish the Children's Missionary Society for education about foreign missions. A new effort in evangelism among African Americans was begun through the pastor's preaching and special meetings. By 1899, the Sabbath school had increased to sixty-six children and adults. The congregation had fifty-two members. The budget for 1899 was $724.21, the largest on record for many years. During his ministry, the session continued to report growth in membership, worship, education and financial support.

Parker left in 1906. Supply pastors served until the congregation called Paul Stanley McChesney in 1908, immediately after he graduated from the Theological Seminary in Columbia. The James Island congregation

Reverend Paul Stanley McChesney, minister, 1908–12. *Archives of Johns Island Presbyterian Church.*

called the Reverend N. Keffer Smith in 1908, and so Johns Island and Wadmalaw Church had its own pastor. During McChesney's ministry, the session was meeting about five times a year, quarterly and on call, to receive new members, to discuss the spiritual condition of the church, to nominate officers to the congregation and to appoint an elder to represent this church at Charleston Presbytery. Occasionally, insights come from the minutes.

The pastor's salary, $750 in a total budget of $1,105, was supported through the Home Mission Committee of the Charleston Presbytery. In addition to maintaining the Sunday school, Mühler's 1912 year-end report for the session recorded, "Our Pastor very often preaches to the Colored people from the Pulpit and by private talks."[115] During McChesney's four-year ministry, the congregation settled in with about forty-seven members, and remained at this number for fifteen years, until the boost that came in the last half of the 1920s under the pastoral and lay leadership of Theodore A. Beckett's ministry.

On May 26, 1912, the congregation met and concurred with McChesney in his request to the Charleston Presbytery that he be free to accept the call of the Presbyterian Church in Kingstree, South Carolina. In December of the same year, the congregation extended a call to Reverend Milton Randolph Kirkpatrick for three-fourths of his time in connection with the Rockville church. The Charleston Presbytery installed him on January 15, 1913, and he served the Presbyterian Church of Johns Island and Wadmalaw until August 1920.

Two elders passed away soon after Kirkpatrick came, and the congregation again sought new leaders. H.C. Mühler, who served as an elder and deacon for eighteen years, died in the spring of 1917. His memorial in the session minutes reads simply, "A Faithful Servant." The minutes after his death were not recorded for almost a year. Mr. John Seabrook wrote as new clerk, "It seems as if our clerk had been in the habit of making notes of meetings in a memorandum book and at the end of the year entering them all at one time. Memorandum book has not been found." The minutes were read annually, during these years, in time for Seabrook to take them to the presbytery meeting in the spring.[116] G.W. Hills also died in late 1914. Thomas S. Legare was elected on March 28, 1915, and ordained by the session after the minister preached "a suitable sermon." Elder Townsend Mikell from Edisto Island Presbyterian Church participated. On April 27, 1919, Theodore A. Beckett Sr. and Lewis H. Hay were ordained and installed as elders. In 1919, the session began to meet monthly.

Although the net membership and annual budgets remained at the same level, newcomers continued to arrive and find their home in the congregation, coming forward to replace the passing members of the previous generation. Kirkpatrick's ministry paved the way for the future well-being of the congregation. Among these names appear a new generation of the families who had been in the congregation for many years, as well as new members coming into the area for the first time. The spouses and children of both long-term families and new residents received the welcome of the pastor and people. This harmony between old family members and new arrivals made for a strong congregation, and the coming years showed many of these names in leadership positions. This welcome development of new leaders set a good example for the rapid changes in the coming years. The congregation needed new strength for its programs, and it welcomed the growth.

Reverend and Mrs. Kirkpatrick encouraged the strengthening of the women's organization. The Johns Island Missionary Society expanded and offered leadership in education of children, fundraising for the pastor's

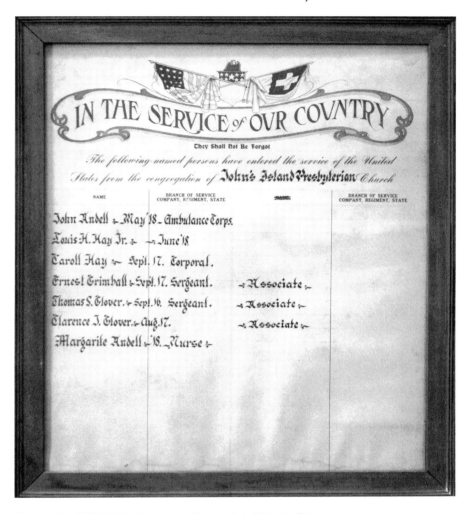

Honor roll of World War I veterans. *Photograph by Katharine Bair.*

salary, missionary education and financial support, congregational care and the mutual fellowship of members. Before women could vote in civil elections or serve as officers in the Presbyterian Church, the women's organization became informed about the Presbyterian denominational programs at home and abroad. It provided vitality and made indispensable contributions to the life of the congregation and services in the Johns Island community. The women's organization was key to the health of the congregation.

The record of the women's organization offers important insight into the life of the church in the early days of the twentieth century, specifically from 1913 to 1919. Like the circle meetings of later Presbyterian women, the monthly meetings were most often held in the homes of members with the hostess and her helpers serving midday dinner. Usually eight to thirteen members attended. Dues were ten cents a meeting. The meetings were opened with prayer, a reading from the Bible and an answer of roll call by quoting a verse. The organization acknowledged the boost by the new pastor, Kirkpatrick; the assignment was for each member to formulate ideas on "how our society might be improved." Eight entries recorded support and suggestions.

There was great appreciation for the president of the women's organization. Resolutions encouraged members to study the program of mission and to dedicate funds to it. It was easier to set aside ten cents a meeting than to collect a dollar at the end of the year. One member wrote:

> *I think our little Missionary Society is doing us a great deal of good; the meetings are truly refreshing, although I really think we could study missions lots more than we do, and we must not let the social part do away with the spiritual, neither must we try to make it a matter of caste, for this is a spiritual meeting and we want to be sisters in Spirit and in truth. Christ the carpenter scorned neither the rich or poor, the high or the low, but in God's name he visited them one and all.*

Mrs. Hay wrote using her maiden name: "Well, it comes rather hard for me to write anything original, as I am a Parrott by nature." She went on to say, "I think we should for the time try to lay aside all thoughts of ourselves and our own little affairs and study about His work and how we can help in it." Another woman suggested, "To improve our Society I suggest that we request Mrs. J.B. Walpole to render an instrumental selection whenever the meeting is held where there is a piano or organ." Mrs. Walpole would have certainly played the old melodeon, which she and Captain Walpole carted to church every Sunday before a pump organ was placed in the sanctuary in the late nineteenth century. Still another member offered:

The melodeon owned by Lydia B. Walpole, which she played for church services. *Courtesy of the Walpole family.*

Our Society in my estimation has improved. Our meetings are large and much more interesting than at first. I think meeting at the homes of the members has been a decided improvement; it brings us together more socially. Now I do think we talk too much during our meetings.

The members met regularly at Rockville and attended presbyterial, the women's organization of the Charleston Presbytery, at various churches:

One echo of the Rockville meeting is the desire of some members to teach colored children the gospel, resulting in the nomination of Mrs. F.Y. Legare and Mrs. T.S. Legare to visit Rev. Thorne, colored Preacher, and see if same is congenial with his Sunday School. The said teaching to be done as the Society work there by giving Society credit for Local Home Work.

In June, Mrs. Legare reported on her interview with Reverend Thorne. He received her favorably, and his Sunday school teachers seconded "that white teachers would be welcome to help teach the Bible." In October, Mrs. Legare reported on work at the Zion Presbyterian Church, "handicapped to some extent for want of literature."[117] The effort in teaching in partnership with the African American congregations came in part as a response to the Presbyterian Church's evangelism program. The African American Presbyterian churches on Johns and Wadmalaw Islands were members of the Atlantic Presbytery in the northern Presbyterian Church, so the cooperation crossed denominational lines. Though racial segregation was both law and social practice, the women carried on the sharing of church work together, responding to the Presbyterian Church's program of evangelism in the African American community.

Toward the end of Kirkpatrick's ministry, in January 1919, the automobile transporting members to their meeting broke down. The women's minutes record:

The regular monthly meeting was scheduled to meet at Mullet Hall this day 3.30 P.M. but owing to a breakdown of the automobile, carrying the President and four members, it was impossible to carry out schedule and it was decided to have our meeting at the Stono School House (a few yards from place of breakdown).

The women continued as usual with singing of hymn, prayer by Mrs. T.S. Legare and roll call answered by names of missionaries in China. At that meeting, there was a report from the secretary of the Charleston Presbyterial on the Johns Island role in financing the work done through its Committee on Colored Work on the Islands. Then "a very peaceful and interesting study" was given by Mrs. J.B. Walpole on Mark 4:3–5:20. A postscript follows: "We take pleasure in welcoming Mrs. Edward Bryan and Mrs. Hamilton's return to the Society's membership." The ladies overcame with a flourish the early car crash and the primitive roadway. From this rich narrative, we can see that the members of the society provided essential leadership for the whole congregation. The congregation and the presbyterial and synodical women's organizations made possible a broad support of the program of the Presbyterian denomination's work in home and foreign missions and in local church and community service.

During his pastorate, Kirkpatrick also continued to build the educational program. In 1915, the session elected T.S. Legare as superintendent of the Sunday school and J.B. Walpole as assistant. Later, Walpole replaced Legare. In 1918, even facing financial challenges, Deacons Lewis H. Hay and J.B. Walpole met jointly with the session to confer about the Presbyterian denomination-wide program to raise $3 million for benevolences. John L. Seabrook became the congregational manager. In 1919, the session named officers of the Sunday school: Mrs. J.E. Andell in charge of home education; Mrs. Kirkpatrick, the cradle roll; G. Walter Hills, superintendent; and J.E. Andell, secretary. The session asked the pastor and the superintendent to choose other teachers.

By the time Kirkpatrick resigned in 1920, the congregation had developed a new cadre of leaders and a cooperative spirit. Even though the membership did not increase in numbers, in commitment of talent and quality of service, new members lived up to the high standards set by the

Presbyterian College campus, 1892. Johns Island Presbyterian Church supported the development of Presbyterian College in Clinton, South Carolina. *Courtesy of Presbyterian College.*

Home of Peace, Thornwell Orphanage, Clinton, South Carolina. The early Presbyterian women's organization contributed to the orphanage and sponsored children. *Courtesy of Presbyterian College.*

longer-term members. A spirit of harmony and good humor comes through in the reports. The cooperation between old families and members with new names is remarkable. In September 1920, "a committee was appointed to be on the lookout for another minister," and the session named elders T.A. Beckett, John Seabrook and Deacon F.Y. Legare, whose father had served so long before him. The congregation was moving into another era. The ministry of Theodore Ashe Beckett brings us to the second main period in the story of the congregation in the twentieth century.

THE MINISTRY OF THEODORE ASHE BECKETT JR., 1924–1945

The congregation called the Reverend Theodore Ashe Beckett on February 24, 1924, and he remained until October 22, 1944, serving into 1945, when he moved to James Island. His length of service was second only to Elipha White (1822–49) a century before. We can see parallels and differences between the two pastors separated by one hundred years. White was a Congregational Church home missionary, educated in New England, who came to Johns Island, married Elizabeth Basnett Legare, daughter of Thomas Legare, and so became a son-in-law of the congregation, as well as its distinguished pastor. Beckett, as a native son of the church who came back to the congregation, was more like John L. Stevens, pastor from 1880 to 1884, also born into the congregation. All three of these members of prominent families led the congregation as its pastors.

Reverend Theodore Ashe Beckett, 1915, when he graduated from Columbia Theological Seminary. *C. Benton Kline Jr. Special Collections and Archives, John Bulow Campbell Library, Columbia Theological Seminary. Used by permission.*

Beckett was born on Johns Island on December 13, 1883, to T.A. Beckett Sr. and Margaret Elizabeth McClung Beckett. He studied at Davidson College from 1908 to 1912, graduating with a bachelor of arts, and at Columbia Theological Seminary from 1913 to 1915, earning a bachelor of divinity. The congregation, especially through the women's organization, contributed toward his education. His wife was Mary Ewing Scroggs from Statesville, North Carolina. They were married on June 3, 1915, and had five children: Mary Ewing (Mrs. E.H. Townsend), Katherine Middleton, Jerome Scroggs, William Wade and Lois Elizabeth. Lois died in childhood, and her grave is in the family plot in the cemetery. Beckett was licensed to preach and ordained in the Charleston Presbytery. His first pastorates were in Whitmire, South Carolina, and Glenn Springs (1915–20). In 1921, he came to North Charleston as an evangelist and became pastor at James Island and Johns Island and Wadmalaw Churches in 1924.

In thinking about the Johns Island and Rockville churches during Beckett's ministry, congregational studies offer useful information about number of members and available resources.[118] A small church of fifty or fewer active members is often called a family church because the mothers and fathers of its prominent families provide the basic leadership for the organization. The role of the pastor in a family church is to lead worship, perhaps teach Bible classes and provide pastoral care for the family members. This designation has to do with not only the size of membership and resources but also the attitude and expectation of the members. When a congregation gains a sufficiently large number of resources and members, usually between 50 and 150, a shift in needs and expectations normally takes place. The congregation then relies more on the pastor because the fathers and mothers are too many to initiate and sustain the life of the congregation on their own. The congregation comes to want a minister who not only provides pastoral care but also directs the organization of the congregation and helps it flourish.

As a home mission congregation, the Johns Island and Wadmalaw Presbyterian Church had at times shared its pastor with James Island and other congregations. The pastor could not lead worship services every Sunday morning in the month. Leadership for worship, fellowships, youth and Sunday school came by the initiative of members. Beckett was a member of the family-sized Johns Island church. During his ministry, the congregation grew, gaining members and resources, and it moved from a family-sized to a pastoral-sized congregation. The transition required different expectations from the members and the pastor. Beckett's great pastoral contribution came from his ability to lead the congregation through the major change in its size and needs and to keep the members' confidence and support. He was able to achieve this through his pastoral gifts, his knowledge and commitments to the people and his long years of consistent and competent leadership of the congregation from the 1920s through the Great Depression and World War II. The enduring gift of his leadership was a stronger congregation that gained its independence by growth in membership, stewardship and service, all the while affirming its partnership and cooperation with the southern Presbyterian denomination.

What was Johns Island like when Beckett came back as pastor? After the boll weevil devastated the South Carolina cotton crop by 1922, causing an early start to financial depression in the state, farming changed. In the first decades of the twentieth century, family farms produced commercial crops of cabbages, white and sweet potatoes, cucumbers, corn, peas and beans. The families employed laborers, mostly African Americans. Timber harvesting and sometimes pecans supplemented the crops. Cattle for beef and milk, hogs and chickens supplied the home and markets. They used mules for wagons and carts and broke wild marsh ponies for riding. When the farm truck and tractor broke down, the mechanic farmer often took the car to Charleston to get parts. Large crops were harvested, put in hampers, crates or barrels and shipped by boat, truck and train to the wholesale markets in Charleston and points beyond. The financial gain was modest. The weather was either a best friend or the worst enemy. Drought or too much rain could diminish or destroy the crops, and sometimes the indebtedness to the suppliers and mercantile companies made the farm economy precarious. With the Great Depression, many farms went out of business or barely survived.

The face of agriculture continued to change with mechanization and the policies of government support, including crop subsidy and land banks during the post-Depression recovery during the presidency of Franklin Delano Roosevelt. By 1945, at the end of Beckett's ministry, the rural economy and way of life had changed. The coming decades would bring larger-scale, corporate truck farming, mechanized and transported on the highway system built after President Dwight Eisenhower's successful promotion of the Interstate Highway System.[119] The mid-twentieth century would bring a new quality and kind of life to Johns Island, and the Johns Island Presbyterian Church would enter a new period of its life.

Lida Beckett Andell and her husband, John Andell, were prominent members of the church. In her diary, Lida gives us indication of the rich family life of many on the island and their joyful participation in the social life of the community.[120] The men hunted deer, birds, raccoon and even possum. They fished for sport and for the table. Lida and her husband gigged flounder, caught channel bass, sheepshead and shark and sometimes netted large mullet. Dances at the Agricultural Hall on Angel Oak Road brought bands from Charleston nearly every week. The Agricultural Hall was on an acre of land donated to the Agricultural Society of Johns Island by George Walter Hills in 1920 and used for farmers' meetings, dances and political rallies and as a temporary school and a WPA sewing room during the Depression.[121] The Johns Island sailboat *Evelyn* frequently took the cup at the Rockville regattas. Picnics, fish fries and oyster roasts brought people together at the Agriculture Hall. Some of the men occasionally went to Clemson football games. Christmas, Easter and Thanksgiving provided seasonal festivities, uniting family, friends and, to a degree, employees. On Sunday after church, the Andell family loved to welcome crowds of visitors to their home or their cabin on the Seabrook Island beach, where the food and company were bountiful.

What was the church like in the 1920s? John L. Seabrook, clerk of session, wrote the annual report in the spring of 1924. The narrative gives a sense of the worship and work of the church as Beckett was returning to his home church to become its pastor:

> *We hold one preaching service each second and fourth Sabbath. Our membership is about forty seven, about 80% attend regularly. We have received one by letter, none by profession. We had an evangelistic meeting during the summer months but we cannot say that as a result there was any special improvement in our spiritual condition. About three fourths of the families hold family worship and a few belong to the Family Altar*

League. We hold four communion services during the year, about 90% of our members attend. They observe the Lord's Day and are very faithful in presenting their children for baptism, and taught the catechism at home and in the Sunday school and some memorize the Scriptures and Hymns. The principles of stewardship of Life and possessions are taught by the Pastor. We are unable to say how many tithe. We conducted a every member canvass and more than paid our apportionment for Benevolences. We paid our Supply (Theological Student) $840. Worldly conformity does not exist to any great extent; we do some evangelistic work among the colored people. No special effort has been made to secure recruits for the ministry. By order of the Session: John L. Seabrook, Clerk.[122]

From this plain-spoken narrative we can see that the congregation had been stable for a long time between regular ministers. Directly before Beckett arrived, a student from the Theological Seminary in Columbia supplied the preaching of the Word. The congregation showed steady and faithful service. The high percentage of attendance demonstrated the loyalty of the members. Church activities were the most regular and important social events for most of the members. The judgment on "worldly conformity," repeated year after year in the narrative reports, was the answer to a question by the Presbyterian denomination about the spirituality of the church, the understanding that members were bound to observe the personal implication of devotion in life and home, that Christian people refrain from "worldly pleasures" and that Christianity primarily had to do with individual life and personal salvation.

Family devotional life was supported by the Family Altar League, and it required express decision and regular spiritual discipline. The evangelistic work among African Americans came from the Christian duty to proclaim the good news of the gospel and to serve the underprivileged members of the community. Sundays were for rest, family life, Christian worship and study. Educational ministry through the Sunday school and the personal and family practices of memorizing the Westminster shorter catechism and Bible passages showed commitment to traditionally strong Presbyterian traditions of discipleship and learning.

The worship and discipline of learning came as a part of the promise of the congregation to children in infant baptism and the sponsorship of young people by the congregation. The financial report showed that the congregation's contribution to the salary of the new pastor was $881. The benevolences showed that giving to the Presbyterian mission was a priority of the congregation, along with Sunday school and the women's organization. When one considers the extent and depth of the worship and work of the Johns Island and Wadmalaw Island congregation in Mr. Seabrook's report compared to the limited resources available to the members, his tone is too modest.

Sometimes the rate of change in the congregation is nearly imperceptible. The years after World War I brought optimism, soon to be dashed by the Great Depression, and the effects of these history-making world events came to Johns Island, too. The decision in 1924 to change the name of the congregation from Johns and Wadmalaw Islands Presbyterian Churches to Johns Island Presbyterian Church was a mark of new aspirations for the independence and initiative of the congregation.[123] The new arrangement was a return to sharing the minister with James Island Presbyterian Church, even though some services at Rockville and the use of the Wadmalaw Island manse continued. In 1928, the session permitted the pastor's family to move from Rockville to "nearer Johns Island Presbyterian Church," and a new manse was purchased.[124] The congregation was moving toward having its pastor give more of his time to serving the church, which had moved beyond a family-led organization to a congregation that needed and wanted a full-time pastor.

The annual reports of the session to the Charleston Presbytery provide a benchmark for viewing the characteristics of the membership through the years. In 1924, John Seabrook's numbers show forty-seven communicant members and a budget of $2,197. The membership and budget began to rise with the leadership of the members and the new pastor for the first seven years, through 1930. In 1926, the session raised its portion of Beckett's pastoral salary from $800 to $1,000. In March 1931, the year-end report showed ninety communicant members and a budget of $3,195, but the congregation was beginning to feel the impact of the Great Depression. Because of members' financial losses and pressure on the church budget, the session asked the presbytery to let its financial commitment to the pastor's salary float in accord with the church's ability to pay. The Charleston

Presbytery, likewise challenged to give support to home mission churches, denied this request. Subsequently, Beckett asked the congregation to reduce its share of his salary back down to $800, which the session gratefully did. Not every minister would have made that offer.

Only men served as elders, but they recognized that the congregation also depended on the leadership of the women in the areas of finance, Christian education and children's work, visitation and care and church hospitality. The Woman's Auxiliary met for fellowship and study in the church, held classes in the evenings and ministered to the newborns, the grieving and the needy outside of the congregation. Lida Beckett Andell and Mrs. F.Y. Legare included a description of the founding and work of the Woman's Auxiliary, which Margaret Adams Gist included in her *Presbyterian Women of South Carolina* (1929). The following excerpt gives details:

> *The Auxiliary was founded in 1920 with three circles and twenty-six members. Mrs. John Andell, President; Mrs. G.S. Legaré, Chairman Circle No. 1; Mrs. G.A. Beckett, Chairman No. 2; Mrs. F.Y. Legaré, Sr., Chairman Circle No. 3 (the old Working Society); Miss Rosa Hay, Vice President; Mrs. R.L. Grimball, Treasurer; Mrs. George Brown, Secretary of Foreign Missions; Mrs. L.H. Hay, Secretary Assembly's Home Missions. They give to all the Assembly's plans and are now buying a manse. All their pastors have encouraged them. The present and largest church membership is fifty-seven.*[125]

The financial support of the Women of the Church is evident in the annual statements reported by the session to the Charleston Presbytery. The congregation, even in the low time of the Great Depression, supported the benevolences of the denomination, and during these years the women's benevolence contribution was from 20 to 36 percent of the contribution of the congregation. Sometimes they contributed more than half of the congregation's share of the pastor's salary. In addition, they raised money for the purchase of the manse on Johns Island. They kept the congregation informed about Presbyterian evangelism at home and abroad. The session supported the women's teaching and, in 1926, named Kenneth W. Leland superintendent and James B. Walpole assistant superintendent to organize the Sabbath school. The women, in their dedication, gave ample evidence for the session members' appreciation and respect for their work.

During Beckett's ministry, six elders died: Ephraim Mikell Seabrook (1837–1926), Thomas S. Legare (1854–1927), John Basnett Walpole (1860–1929), John Lewis Seabrook (1877–1936), Eugene Gordon Hay (1857–1936) and Lewis Holding Hay (1867–1940). The session dedicated a page of the minute book to their memory, usually including a sketch of a memorial stone, with dates and a written record of thanksgiving, which was sent to the family and the *Christian Observer*, an independent Presbyterian magazine. Some of the memorials are in a style that is liable to seem too flowery to us, but they are sincere, and they often offer particularly touching remembrances.

Of E.M. Seabrook, the oldest of these, the session wrote, in part:

> *On Friday evening October 1ˢᵗ 1926 our Senior Elder Ephraim Mikell Seabrook was called by the Angel of death from Earth to sit with the Elders above. Brother Seabrook was for nineteen years Elder in the Johns Island Presbyterian Church, having been elected to that office October 25, 1907. He lived to the ripe old age of eighty nine years. He belonged to [a] period in and type of our civilization fast passing away.*[126]

The memorial to J.B. Walpole in January 1929, expressed appreciation for his service as deacon and elder, particularly for his interest in the Sunday school as assistant and superintendent from 1915 to 1929:

> *On every side we hear, "his place will be hard to fill." He exemplified the injunction, "Be faithful in all things" and in the Sunday School, in the service of song, in the details of decent and orderly procedure of the church service, he was always faithful. He was loyal and devoted to his pastor and allowed no criticism of men of God in his presence. An affectionate and considerate husband and father. God give us more of his kind.*[127]

It could equally have been said of all of these men that they "belonged to a period in and type of our civilization fast passing away." Captain E.M. Seabrook was a Confederate officer, was wounded and served with distinction. John L. Seabrook was his son, born on Johns Island during Reconstruction. When he died in 1936, the memorial read:

> *John L. Seabrook was born on Johns Island February 8, 1877. He as a son of the late E.M. Seabrook, an honored elder of our Church, and had the rare privilege of being set apart to the eldership by the laying on of hands of the Session, his father participating in the service, when only twenty-six years of age. He was clerk of the Session from February 10, 1918 to the time of his death and often his work as clerk was publicly commended to the Presbytery. He was a man of high principle; a true friend; a father and husband of the highest type, and exemplified in his life the fine traditions of an honored name. We miss him as a friend, presbyter, clerk of Session and citizen. We commend his example to those who come after him.*[128]

A space but no written memorial appears in the minutes for Eugene Gordon Hay (July 15, 1857–April 16, 1936), but a particularly beautiful memorial is recorded for Lewis Holding Hay (September 29, 1867–March 25, 1940):

> *Lewis Holding Hay was born at Varnville, September 29, 1867, died on Wadmalaw Island, March 25, 1940.*
>
> *He served as an officer of our Church for thirty years: Deacon from September 18, 1910 to April 27, 1919, when he was elected and ordained to the eldership. He was faithful to his trust; delicate in his advice; above reproach in his life, a constant source of comfort to the needy, exemplifying liberal, cheerful giving; a friend to his pastor, and a wise, loving husband and father. He was humble in his faith, not articulate in its expression, but honored, loved and respected for his warm generosity and high integrity. We miss him and shall miss him. Truly his works and his example live to minister among us on earth while he enjoys his heavenly reward in the inheritance not made with hands, eternal in the heavens.*

These memorials show us the genuine feeling of the members of the congregation. These long-serving elders, elected to serve until they died, gained the trust and affection of the people. They came from or immediately after the Civil War era. In most cases, they were first elected deacons as young men and served through several pastoral terms, giving continuity and stability to the congregation. The passing of these elders would require a new generation to bring their own judgments and commitments while they remembered and preserved the inheritance of the bygone era.

The Sunday school was central in the life of the church. It met in assembly for worship and study and took up an offering every Sunday, even when there were no "preaching services." In 1930, Mrs. John E. Andell, historian of the Woman's Auxiliary, wrote about the educational program. She reported on the work of Sarah Gray, "our island worker" appointed by the Synod of South Carolina to work in education and care. She held Sunday school classes and taught sewing, working with Zion Presbyterian Church. Young people attended conferences, and in 1929, Reverend Beckett took several youth to Presbyterian College in June: Evelyn Limehouse and Walter Hills were intermediates; E.B. Hay and Sam Seabrook were members of the young people. In 1930, the women organized Christian Endeavor, an interdenominational youth ministry; Mrs. Andell wrote:

> *The Sunday School has been particularly flourishing this year. Several families have made it their business to bring neglected children, and in this way some of our new and less fortunate neighbors are being reached with Christian training.*[129]

Kenneth Leland's service as superintendent lasted until 1935; E.S. Dukes took his place. Because of its importance, even though the church was financially strapped by the Great Depression, in November 1933 the session approved a request by the Woman's Auxiliary for an investigation of "some changes in the church to accommodate some of the Sunday School classes."[130] The next summer, the congregation began fundraising for the Sunday school building and sold timber off the property for fifty dollars. In the spring of 1936, a committee of women reported on the building; these leaders were Mrs. W.C. Hills, Mrs. T.A. Beckett and Mrs. Lena Legare. They urged special attention and giving for the Sunday school, even when it was financially difficult.[131] The determination of the members to provide for an expanding Sunday school enrollment and increase in classes came in part

Memorial to Reverend Theodore Ashe Beckett Jr. (1883–1961). *Photograph by Katharine Bair.*

because the educational ministry offered good leadership for growth. Also, they wanted to provide for continuity in gathering families on Sundays when no minister was available.

In 1934, Beckett requested, and the session granted, a leave to go to Memphis for several months for major surgery and convalescence. Seven months later, the pastor took leave to return to the hospital for a month at his own expense. He left Johns Island Presbyterian Church in 1944 and continued to serve the James Island Presbyterian Church.[132] The record for the twenty-one years of Beckett's ministry shows that 136 or more persons became members. Many of these were children of the families of the church who grew up on the island and came to the session for membership. They came and offered a new generation of participation and leadership, and some of their children and grandchildren would follow them in the coming years. However, new families also came, preparing the way for another chapter in the story of the congregation.

MID-TWENTIETH CENTURY

After T.A. Beckett's twenty-year pastoral service, the next two decades brought five pastors into the service of Johns Island Presbyterian Church:

James H. Taylor (supply), 1945–1946
W.B. Gaston, 1947–1951
Gaston Boyle, 1951–1955
John R. Williams, 1956–1959
R. Wilbur Cousar, 1960–1965

The Reverend Dr. James H. Taylor acted as a supply minister from September 1945 to August 1946. He was born in Charleston in 1871, and he returned in 1943 after retiring as pastor emeritus from Central Presbyterian Church in Washington, where he served for thirty-seven years. President and Mrs. Woodrow Wilson worshiped in his congregation from 1913 to 1924. Dr. Taylor was educated at Phillips Academy, Yale University (BA, 1894), Columbia Theological Seminary and Louisville Presbyterian

Theological Seminary (BD, 1897).[133] This distinguished pastor gave able service to the Johns Island Presbyterian Church. He led the congregation in denominational programs; for example, an annual week of self-denial for home missions. The congregation raised its seventy-five-dollar quota.[134] He encouraged the leadership of the Young Peoples' League, and when Mrs. Kenneth Leland resigned as adviser, the session appointed Mrs. Eugene Walpole. He instructed the young people for church membership in 1945: Edward LaRoche Hay, Thomas Seabrook Legare, Marty Ellen Davis, Mildred Louise Heaton, James Miley Davis and Bryan Legare Walpole Jr. He diligently called joint officers' meetings of the elders and deacons, while helping the session keep up with its responsibilities.

The officers continuing during Taylor's interim ministry were:

ELDERS
T.A. Beckett Sr.
D.E. Hay
G.W. Hills
W.C. Hills
Kenneth Leland
Vardell Legare

DEACONS
John E. Andell
Henry Hay
S.L. Hay
Bryan Walpole

Near the end of Taylor's time, on April 14, 1946, Theodore Ashe Beckett Sr. resigned as clerk of session. He was born on July 15, 1855, and died in March 1947 at the age of ninety-two. He had served as elder since his ordination on April 27, 1919, and became clerk when John Seabrook died in 1936. The session elected Mr. E.V. Legare to replace him.

Even though the congregation appreciated the interim service Taylor offered, it still had not fully regained its momentum since the interruption caused by Beckett's departure for James Island in 1945. Furthermore, the

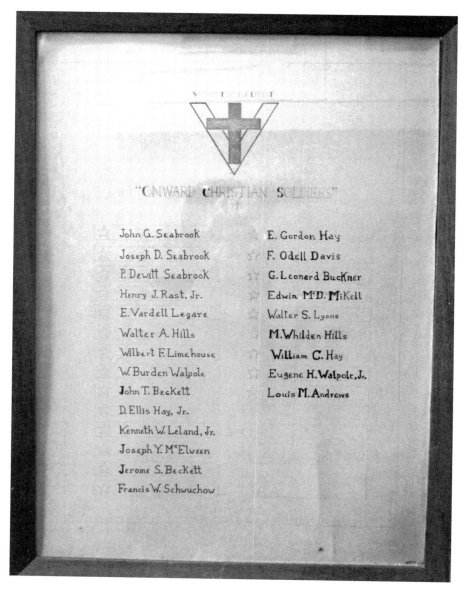

Honor roll of World War II veterans. *Photograph by Katharine Bair.*

victory of World War II and the beginning of the prospect of greater prosperity in its wake also changed the playing field on Johns Island. The church faced a degree of change to which it was not accustomed. In March 1946, a joint meeting of elders and deacons heard from T.A. Jamieson, Edmund Seabrook and E.H. Townsend, from the Rockville congregation, who offered to unite the congregations in calling a minister. The congregation agreed, and Rockville contributed $400 toward the salary and contributed toward the purchase of property for a manse. In July 1946, the congregation elected a nominating committee to recommend a full-time pastor. W.C. Hills, E.V. Legare and K.W. Leland represented the session; S.L. Hay and H.M. Hay represented the diaconate, with a slot for someone from the Woman's Auxiliary.

The committee received a number of names from the list of chaplains from the Military Service Council. It reported on April 20, 1947; the congregation elected the Reverend William Bartlett Gaston, pastor of the First Presbyterian Church in Montevallo, Alabama, as its pastor. Gaston was originally from Aberdeen, North Carolina. He and his wife, Aline D. Jones, from Richmond, Virginia, had a son, William B. Jr., and a daughter, Aline Drake. The pastor graduated from the University of South Carolina (BS, 1938) and Union Theological Seminary in Virginia (BD, 1943). Mrs. Gaston joined the membership at Johns Island on September 26, 1946.

After World War II ended, new names began to appear among the members. Gaston's 1947 communicants' class brought the following youth into the church: Lane Barnwell, William Sydney Howell, Frances Murrell Howell, Horace Edward Walpole, Marthaanne Limehouse, Mary Scott Walpole, Betty Awanda Barnwell, Elizabeth Anne Davis and George Peter Oesterkamp.[135] Later generations of children represented the old families, but new ones were also coming into the congregation. Members from longtime Johns Island families were dispersing to other places. Joseph Dill and Paul D. Seabrook were dismissed to the Walterboro Church, and Mr. and Mrs. T.A. Beckett III moved to the Second Presbyterian Church in Charleston. New families joined; for example, Dr. and Mrs. Ralph S. Wager came from the First Baptist Church in Decatur, Georgia. The elders seemed delighted to welcome new members, and they gave Dr. and Mrs. Wager "the right hand of welcome and fellowship." Both the dispersion of long-term family members and the welcome of new members would increase in the coming years.[136]

Gaston gathered the elders and deacons in joint session every quarter. These joint meetings of the officers considered initiatives—sometimes from the pastor, sometimes from the members—for the good of the congregation,

Reverend William Bartlett Gaston, minister, 1947–51. *Archives of the William Smith Morton Library, Union Theological Seminary and Presbyterian School of Christian Education. Used by permission.*

and the minutes reflect thoughtful decisions. The pastor recommended adding morning worship on fifth Sundays of the month, since no preaching occurred on this day when he was responsible for the Wadmalaw Island Church service. The session wanted to ask Dr. Taylor to return; this was not a good idea. The officers discussed a visitation evangelism program in cooperation with the Charleston Presbytery and set a plan for a series of evangelistic services in March 1948. Gaston led the session to call for an organization of the Men of the Church and invited the Rockville Church to participate. He also asked the session to change the method of serving Communion, but the elders decided to make no changes.[137]

The elders wanted the Sunday morning schedule carefully observed and instructed the pastor, church organist, Mrs. John Limehouse and the Sunday school superintendant, Samuel G. Seabrook, "to make every effort to have Sunday School end at 11:55 AM and church service begin by 12:05 PM." Also, the treasurer was instructed to give quarterly financial reports, beginning with the church year April 1948 to March 1949. Church bulletins were approved for use at the pastor's discretion. Despite the stern instruction for the Sunday morning schedule, the officers warmly supported the pastor, the Sunday school and the music program. When the organ needed repair the following November, E.V. Legare joined with a committee to look into repair or replacement, and the matter was turned over to the deacons and the Men of the Church for action. Soon, Mrs. Limehouse, the organist, was received into the membership. At last, at the joint meeting of the officers in 1949, the session finally agreed to participate more actively in the service of Communion, with an elder helping to remove the table-covering cloth from the elements and replacing it after the service. With W.B. Gaston as their new pastor, the officers approved the statistical report at the end of 1947: 123 active members; benevolence giving, $4,552; and local church expenses, $6,024, for a total budget of $10,576.

The congregation received a boost from the post–World War II growth coming to the area.[138] The church was developing new program energy and expanding facilities. It increasingly participated in the program of the larger denomination through the Synod of South Carolina and the Charleston Presbytery. The denomination's Program of Progress emphasis for foreign missions was noted, and the officers set a date for the Reverend Leslie Patterson to address the congregation in January 1949. The Men of the Church sponsored a "Prove God Period" for the budget season and requested that the pastor preach on tithing to introduce the emphasis, which was to continue from January into April 1949. The men were quite active, and when the Reverend David A. McLean, missionary to Africa, came for the mission emphasis season in January, the Men of the Church invited the whole congregation.

The officers also promoted evangelism on Johns Island through visitation, set for April in cooperation with the synod's home mission emphasis. Church families were asked to pray together for fifteen minutes each night of the visitation campaign, from April 3 to 7, 1949. The next year, quarterly treasurer reports came to the congregation, giving information on the pledges and the receipts toward budget. The joint officers meeting considered the membership of the church, and the session authorized retiring inactive members. The officers approved that all persons and organizations contribute to the Fellowship Building Fund to erect a separate building on church property to house a meeting room and other features. Mrs. George W. Hills was elected treasurer of the fellowship hall building program. In the summer of 1950, Sunday school was suspended because of the polio epidemic, but the enthusiasm and support for the new education building carried the day.

Again, the congregation lost a beloved member and elder with the death of George Walter Hills on November 19, 1950. He was received into the membership on January 12, 1896, on certificate. He was elected by the congregation, along with W.C. Hills, on April 26, 1936.[139] The pastor wrote a memorial for the congregation and the family:

> On November 19, 1950, G.W. Hills, a long time member and for fourteen years an elder of the Johns Island Presbyterian Church departed this life. He was a better than ordinary farmer and business man. His standing in the community was of the highest, reflecting credit on his faith and bringing glory to the Lord who he professed to serve. His public spiritedness may be judged by the fact that the day before his final illness struck him, he went to the polls to cast his ballot. He combined, to an unusual degree, the wisdom of years and a youthful zest for life, taking the keenest pleasure in simple things. He was a loving and devoted husband, and a splendid example to his five children, all of whom have taken places in community and church life. Mr. Hills was by nature retiring but his friendly smile and warm hand-clasp and his genuine interest in people endeared him to the hearts of close friends and casual acquaintances alike. His seat in church was never vacant except for sickness of himself or his family. He was a frequent attendant at the higher courts of his church. Mr. Walter Hills will be greatly missed, but his life will continue to up lift and strengthen those who knew and loved him.

Near the end of his third year of service, Gaston asked the session to call a congregational meeting for December 10, 1950, to approve the Charleston Presbytery's permission for him to accept another call. On Christmas Eve, before he left, Mr. Gaston presided over the reception of young people and newcomers into the congregation and led the ordination and installation of new officers: Elders L.H. Hay and J.S. Wallace and Deacon W.B. Seabrook.[140] On December 17, 1950, the congregation elected a committee to seek a new pastor.

Five months later, in May 1951, the Reverend Gaston Boyle Jr. was nominated and called by the acclamation of the congregation at Johns Island Presbyterian Church. He was born to Presbyterian missionaries in Brazil on October 28, 1917. He married Mary Virginia Stegall from Steele's Tavern, Virginia, on May 22, 1946, and they had three daughters, Mary Kathleen, Judith Anne and Elizabeth Susan. He graduated from Hamden-Sidney College (BA, 1940) and Union Theological Seminary in Virginia (BD, 1949). His four-year ministry was brief, in part because of controversy over his support of the reunion of the northern and southern Presbyterian Churches in 1954 and his open support of teaching about race relations in the year of the United States Supreme Court *Brown v. Board of Education* decision, which declared that segregated schools were unconstitutional. However, his leadership inspired the congregation in evangelism, new membership and a plan for the construction of an educational building. He left plans in place that the session and Dr. R.

Reverend Gaston Boyle Jr., minister, 1951–55. *Archives of the William Smith Morton Library, Union Theological Seminary and Presbyterian School of Christian Education. Used by permission.*

Wilbur Cousar, the next pastor, used effectively. The congregation grew in numbers and strength while Boyle was minister.

Through the changes of pastors, the members of the congregation kept to their plans to build a manse and education facilities. Before Boyle came, the session had already called for the raising of $6,500 to complete the manse. The Rockville church was given the opportunity to participate. If funds over the amount could be obtained, they would be designated for the educational building. In November 1952, the Boyle family moved into the new manse on the property adjoining the church.[141] In June 1953, with the solid support of the congregation in giving and affirmation, a committee to plan an educational building selected a site plan, and on January 25, 1954, the congregation approved the plan presented by Mr. Lewis Hay. He reported in March that the building committee had about $9,000 on hand and recommended commencing the building in July 1954.[142] Mr. Louis Andrews and Mr. Allen Klinger were to be in charge of construction, with some of the work to be done by members and other work to be done by subcontract.

Boyle was attentive to teaching and leading the congregation in evangelism and mission. His birth in the field and his personal theology gave him a strong sense of the evangelical mission of the church. In July 1952, the session set a series of evangelistic meetings for September. The pastor was asked to secure a preacher. Boyle presented World Mission addresses in late January 1953, the Presbyterian season of mission emphasis. In the spring of 1953, the congregation repeated special evangelistic services for the congregation and visitors. Boyle was invited to preach in First (Scots) Presbyterian Church by Dr. Edward Lilly, and St. Johns Episcopal Church invited him to teach a weekly Bible class in its school. He also held an adult evening class one Sunday a month.[143] The congregation approved a rotation plan for the diaconate, and the session urged the minister to train newly elected deacons. It set a six-week program, and the curriculum included the Westminster Confession and a denominational book, *Presbyterians in Action*.[144]

By 1953, Sunday school enrollment had reached 132. Youth fellowship was active, and in 1954, Mrs. Winnie Hay and Mrs. J.S. Wallace were appointed youth leaders for the Presbyterian Youth Fellowship and Pioneers. The congregation needed new educational classrooms. However, in June 1954 the project was delayed for two months while the session studied "the possible effects of the Assembly's action on segregation."[145] In August, it was delayed again, and the pastor conducted a series of prayer meetings. Building was delayed until January 1955, when the presbytery would vote on church reunion. The proposal for Presbyterian reunion failed. On April 5, 1955, the session granted permission to the building committee to proceed with the educational building construction. In August 1955, Mr. Boyle appointed a Christian Education Committee including Bryan Walpole, Mr. J.S. Townsend, Mrs. W.B. Seabrook, Mrs. Jack Fowler and Henry Hay. Their duties were to assist the session in serving officers and teachers, to help coordinate the educational program of the church and to study educational programs and recommend changes and improvements.[146]

In October 1954, Boyle presented the Presbyterian three-year commitment program, "Forward with Christ." He suggested the following goals for the congregation:

1. *Growth by 20 new members*
2. *Fifty percent increase in church attendance at worship*
3. *Substantial increase in Church School enrollment*
4. *A definite plan for World Mission*
5. *Presentation of the challenge of World Mission to our young people*
6. *An emphasis on tithing*
7. *An increase of $1,000 in the budget for current expenses*
8. *An increase of $1,000 toward benevolences.*

To pursue these goals, the session would set another series of evangelistic services in March 1955.[147] The program was to include a plan of visitation by elders; membership evangelistic visitation; keeping records of attendance at worship services, church school and visits; letters and cards to the inactive members; quarterly missionary programs; every-member canvass; the implementation of the deacons' manual; the employment of a part-time secretary; a publicity budget; a nursery for children; and monthly meetings of the session to respond and build on the program. The session approved the plan, urging minimizing organizational additions but budgeting $2,000, and requesting a definite plan of action for the next year for its approval. Mrs. W.B. Seabrook was employed four hours a week to assist in the church office.

The controversy over the General Assembly plan for reuniting the northern and southern Presbyterian Churches brought discord into the congregation. Boyle spoke from conscientious conviction and supported the reunion, but he was in the minority in the Charleston Presbytery. In October 1953, the session granted a request of the pastor to distribute denominational literature for and against church reunion. A meeting was set in March or April 1954, with Dr. Edward Lilly, minister of First (Scots) Presbyterian Church, as moderator, the Reverend Thomas Horton to speak against and the Reverend Francis Mayes to present the case for church union.

In January 1955, the session adopted the following affirmation:

> *We agree with the historic position of the Presbyterian Church, which allows and expects its minister of the Word to expound and apply that Word as their conscience dictates so long as that preaching is not contrary to the Word of God as it is understood and interpreted in our Confession of Faith.*[148]

In August 1955, Boyle asked for approval to offer a series of classes on Sunday nights during October on "Scripture and Race Relations." With only two favorable votes, the request was denied.

Apparently, Boyle took the denial as a rejection of his leadership, and in October he asked the session to call a congregational meeting so that he could accept another call. The meeting was held on October 30, 1955. Before he left, he presided at a congregational meeting on November 20 to approve the budget and at a later one on December 2 to elect a pastor-nominating committee.[149] In 1955, the active communicant membership was 161. The budget of $9,277 was down considerably from the previous year, partly because the building project was delayed. However, during Boyle's ministry, the congregation grew in membership and passed a new threshold. With more than 150 active members, it required a more effective organization of volunteers, like the Forward with Christ objectives Boyle had suggested and the elders approved. The larger church needed more programs to attract members and to offer the worship, education and care they needed. Boyle's vision and leadership helped the church attain a new level of programming in response to new opportunities for its ministry on Johns Island. He left on a gracious note.

The transition to a new minister was short. On Sunday, January 1, 1956, the congregation called the Reverend John R. Williams to be the next minister. He came from the Presbyterian Church in Montreat, and he had served as a pastor and evangelist in Virginia, Georgia, South Carolina and Texas since he gained a diploma from Union Theological Seminary in Virginia in 1921. Meeting with the session in March, the elders prepared for his reception into the presbytery and his installation by a commission on March 25, 1956.

The three years of his pastorate were quiet. The controversies associated with Gaston Boyle's ministry subsided, and the session delayed action on organizational plans that it had approved for the Forward with Christ program but soon began to implement some of the plans Boyle had suggested. During the pastorate of Williams, from 1956 to 1959, the congregation continued to grow with new members and budget increases. By the end of 1956, membership had grown to 173, more than half of the goal that the session had approved under Boyle, and the total budget was $17,719. In 1958, membership reached 180, and the gifts to various causes were $15,635.

While Williams was pastor, the officers actively made plans for new program organization. The congregation became larger and busier. The Christian education program found new energy in the greater enrollment and the new building. The session approved a manual for the church school, and in December 1959, the Christian Education Committee was elected and included officers and lay members, men and women. Mr. and Mrs. L.H. Hay and Mrs. Henry Rast led the committee. Aaron Leland was elected assistant superintendant of the Sunday school, and in January 1960, the session elected J.S. Momier as secretary and Don Davis as treasurer of the Sunday school. Dr. Felix Nepveux was appointed advisor to the senior high fellowship. Mrs. L.H. Hay also served as the church librarian. At the request of the Woman's Auxiliary, a committee was asked to preserve "the historical features of the church." The historical committee—H.M. Hay, Mrs. T.C. McDermid and Mrs. B.L. Walpole—was appointed for a two-year term. These committees are examples of the way the congregation moved to accommodate its new program needs. They were composed of both officers and lay people. Even though the congregation did not elect female officers at the time, both women and men served together on these session-appointed committees. A manual guided the committee operations, and terms of office became normal. This organizational pattern became standard for the future.

When pastors serve less than five years, a church does not usually make substantial organizational changes or develop lasting programmatic initiatives.[150] Congregations take time to develop trust in the new pastor and the new configurations of leadership that come with the new relationship. Particularly after a period of stress, the congregation will require a healthy interim. The Johns Island congregation was an exception to the norm during the pastorate of Williams. It grew in membership and stewardship of resources, and it developed strong new organization. Williams was an effective leader. The officers and members were responding vigorously to the growing opportunity for the congregation on Johns Island. Williams remained as pastor until he retired from active ministry on April 12, 1959. The congregation expressed gratitude for his ministry in a tribute mounted on the wall of the church sanctuary.

Dr. R. Wilbur Cousar was called as pastor, and the congregation set his installation for June 5, 1960. He was a native of Bishopville, South Carolina. His wife was Nellie Irving Blanton from Farmville, Virginia, and they had three sons: Robert W. Jr., a Presbyterian minister; J. Burton, a businessman; and Charles B. Cousar, professor of the New Testament at Columbia Theological Seminary. Dr. R. Wilbur Cousar graduated from Davidson College (BA, 1918), Union Theological Seminary in Virginia (BD, 1922; ThM, 1937; ThD, 1941) and served important churches in Virginia, Tennessee and North Carolina. King College awarded him an honorary doctorate of divinity in 1940.

Bringing long years of experience in ministry and a deep commitment, Cousar was a strong leader, encouraging the officers and members of the congregation to move ahead in the momentum that the church had gained responding to the growth of the Johns Island community. He encouraged a new quality of leadership, starting the moment he arrived, and he continued to provide welcome strength throughout his tenure.

He emphasized the support of specific missionaries. At his first session meeting on March 13, 1960, the session approved a donation of $300 to purchase a generator for a mission in Africa. The session met again three

Memorial to Reverend John R. Williams (1893–1964). *Photograph by Katharine Bair.*

Reverend Dr. R. Wilbur Cousar, minister, 1960–65. *Courtesy of Dr. and Mrs. Charles B. Cousar.*

weeks later. The new pastor and the session members discussed the church's needs and set a priority on strengthening the program of Christian education. The elders approved membership visitation to increase Sunday school attendance. In May, the session selected James Beckett to chair a committee to encourage more young people to attend Sunday school and authorized him to appoint a visitation committee. In October, the session approved Mr. and Mrs. Beckett as leaders of a new Pioneer Youth Fellowship. Leonard and Betty Buckner were approved as senior high leaders. In August, the session sent a resolution of thanks to Mr. Cowan W. Toole, the father of Mr. Max G. Toole of Maryville, Tennessee, to thank him for making and giving a lectern, which was placed in the educational building. The gift was in gratitude for "the spiritual and fraternal friendship of the many members of this church for his son Max G. Toole."[151] These details show that Cousar emphasized educational ministry, brought new members into the program and encouraged them.

Meanwhile, the matter of race relations came up again. On September 26, 1960, the session considered "what to do when or if colored people came to church." The session reported that after considering several plans, it was decided "if the colored people come they should be permitted to enter the church, and the ushers should give them any suitable or available seat, preferably alone, if possible." In October, the session received a petition from a number of members "expressing dissatisfaction with the action of the Session." The elders notified the petitioners that, if they wished, they could ask the session to call a congregational meeting to consider their concerns, but they were not permitted to do so under Presbyterian order. The elders also explained that the congregation could not vote on an action by the session, but they could ask that the matter be reconsidered. No more came from the petition.[152] Good use of church order defused the potential conflict.

The session proposed a special program to recognize the 250th anniversary of the congregation, and in May it called for a congregational meeting on June 3, 1960, to plan a fall celebration. With preparation by a committee, the congregation rejoiced in its heritage in a September homecoming. The occasion was a memorable event in which the congregation gave thanks for its two and a half centuries of continuous life and looked ahead to the next years of ministry. Mrs. W.C. (Isabel Lofton) Hills, having long experience as the Women of the Church historian, wrote a very nice summary of the church's story. In October, the session sent her a resolution of thanks for "the excellent history of the church"; it also sent a resolution to Mr. and Mrs. Henry Rast for directing the 250th anniversary celebration.

Cousar continued to build on the initiatives strengthening the ministry of worship through his gifts of preaching and teaching. In the September 1960 session meeting, he read from Ephesians and encouraged the elders to understand their responsibility for the spiritual welfare of the congregation. The session moved forward with a plan for evangelistic services. W.C. Hay and Felix Nepveux were appointed co-chairmen of the Cavalcade of Evangelism. Later in the fall, during stewardship season, Cousar presented the causes of the denomination to a joint meeting of the deacons and the elders, and part of the session's approval of the budget of $5,000 was designated for benevolences above the congregational level in the Charleston Presbytery, the Synod of South Carolina and the General Assembly of the Presbyterian Church. In October, the session called the congregation to meet, and on December 4, 1960, it elected Elders George W. Hills, Walter A. Hills and W.B. Seabrook. On December 16, 1960, the session acted on the emphasis on evangelism and moved to invite Dr. Manford George Gutzke to lead evangelistic services within the year. Dr. Cousar appointed committees to organize the session and charged the chairs to gather appropriate members to lead the work of the congregation:

> *Welcoming Committee, W.B. Seabrook*
> *Christian Education, Walter A. Hills*
> *Evangelistic Committee, L.H. Hay*
> *World Missions Committee, K.W. Leland and E.V. Legare*
> *Church Roll, George W. Hills*

At the minister's suggestion, the session approved in January 1961 a Good Friday evening Communion service and discussed further plans for another series of evangelistic services, which they referred to the evangelism committee, with L.H. Hay as chairman. The other committees began to meet. George W. Hills gave the nine elders a list of names of members to contact to inquire about their church membership, to see if they had moved and to obtain current addresses. At a joint meeting of the officers, the deacons were authorized to install five additional pews in the church.[153] In July 1961, Cousar suggested having an organized prayer group, and the session approved it. Mrs. L.S. Hay's offer to purchase new pulpit chairs was authorized, with the request that the historical committee approve the selection.[154] The former minister, John R. Williams, was invited to conduct services, and the session appointed subcommittees for the event:

> *General Chairmen: Walter Hills and L.H. Hay*
> *Financial: Henry Rast, Chair and B.W. Davis, Assistant*
> *Arrangements and Ushers: Deacons*
> *Music: Mrs. J.P. Limehouse, Chairman, J.A. Beckett, Mrs. B.W. Davis*
> *Spiritual Preparation: Mr. and Mrs. G.W. Hills, Mr. and Mrs. E.H. Walpole Jr.*
> *Publicity Committee: Mr. and Mrs. Max Toole, Mr. and Mrs. Henry Rast, Mr. and Mrs. J.R. Koger Entertainment Committee: Mr. and Mrs. W.B. Seabrook*

This effort was important, and the preparation for it was well developed. From 1962 to 1966, as the congregation reached and exceeded two hundred active members, the pastor and elder leadership recruited broader participation by the members. The congregation celebrated its heritage; looked to the future with effective plans to increase the number of worship services, enlarge the seating in the sanctuary, develop evangelistic services and attract new members; and contributed to local needs, as well as to the mission of the Presbyterian denomination. This new energy and quality of program life helped the congregation continue its development. When Dr. Cousar was honorably retired from active ministry on June 1, 1965, he left the Johns Island Presbyterian Church a stronger congregation. His gifts came from a lifetime of commitment to the Christian faith and many years of distinguished pastoral service. The members of the congregation were grateful to him and to Mrs. Cousar.

After nearly two years in an interim without a full-time pastor, on Sunday, March 26, 1967, the congregation met to hear a report from the nominating committee and to act on the calling of a minister. Mr. Henry Hay, chairman of the committee, placed the Reverend Fielding Russell for election as the next pastor of Johns Island Presbyterian Church. He was elected by an overwhelming majority of the sixty-nine members present and voting. He came from Geneva, Alabama, after serving several pastorates in Georgia and other points in Alabama. He was born in 1932 and was a graduate of Davidson College and Columbia Theological Seminary. He had two uncles who were Presbyterian ministers, and he was the nephew of Senator Richard Russell of Georgia. He was married and had a daughter and a son. The executive secretary of his presbytery in Alabama highly recommended him; he had been particularly active in young people's work. The congregation agreed to pay him a $7,000 salary with annuity and insurance and to provide a manse, utilities and moving expenses for the Russell family. The manse was repaired by using the legacy of Miss A.N. Allan.[155]

The main business of the session during Russell's ministry was to receive and dismiss members, to institute a new system of elder and deacon rotation and to keep and revise the regulations for the cemetery. Growth of membership and the stewardship of financial resources were not as proportionately strong as members hoped.[156] The deacons, concerned about the budget, studied the giving of the church in October 1967. The session changed the worship hour from 11:30 a.m. to 11:00 a.m. and Sunday school from 10:30 a.m. to 10:00 a.m. And the session studied ways to increase attendance and restore inactive members.[157] As always, elders attended presbytery and synod meetings regularly, often electing W.B. Seabrook, J.A. Beckett and L.H. Hay as representatives. The Women of the Church provided regular and strong programs through the circles.

The pastor was particularly interested in youth. In April 1968, he attended a training program in outdoor ministry. He preached at the baccalaureate at Georgia Southern University and helped lead youth rally meetings in the Charleston Presbytery. The youth group from Rockville joined with the Johns Island group in October 1969. The Christian education program was given strength by strong superintendents—H.M. Hay, Aaron Leland and Frances Schwuchow (treasurer).[158] Circle 1 of the Women of the Church requested an assembly to gather the Sunday school at the beginning of the hour.[159] The two children's classes, primary and junior II, were divided according to grade level, and more teachers were added for the additional classes. The lay leadership of the educational program remained strong from previous years of growth.

Keeping support of Presbyterian causes remained important for the congregation. The session invited Reverend Dr. Charles Cousar, son of the previous minister and professor of the New Testament, to lead classes and preach on Columbia Seminary Sunday.[160] The support of missionaries and the witness season programs continued. A program on the crusade for cancer was given by Dr. John C. Hawk of the Medical University of South Carolina. The Presbyterian College development Excel Program received support in 1970. Fellowship suppers brought speakers for denominational programs, including a speaker for Expo '72 and the Key '73 Evangelism program. At year's end, the session called a congregational meeting for December 31, 1972.[161] At Russell's request, the Reverend Charles J. Hollingsworth, associate executive secretary of the Charleston Presbytery, served as moderator. The minister asked to be released from his relationship with Johns Island Presbyterian Church, and the congregation reluctantly granted in his request.

When Fielding Russell left, the congregation received assistance in planning for the election of a pastor-nominating committee from the

Charleston Presbytery Commission on the Minister and His Work. Officers and members of the Johns Island church met over a period of several months with representatives of the presbytery to strengthen its witness. The session approved a questionnaire for surveying the members and used the information for a time of setting goals for a good way forward. The Reverend Thomas Horton, executive secretary of the Charleston Presbytery, and the associate gave a program and met with the elders and deacons in a goal-setting day. A congregational visitation in June was chaired by Aaron Leland.[162] The outcome was a strong recommendation for provisions for the calling of a new minister, including "quite a lot of work" to repair the manse.

The session called a congregational meeting on February 25, 1973, to elect a pastor-nominating committee and asked Hollingsworth to preside. After determining that the committee would serve for one year, the following nominees were elected from the floor with a view to represent broadly the congregation:

> *From the Session, George Hills*
> *From the Deacons, Legare Walpole*
> *From the Women of the Church, Mrs. Jack Fowler*
> *At large from the congregation, Leonard Buckner*
> *From the Senior Highs, Billy Hay*

New Directions, 1975–2003

The nominating committee achieved its task within the year. At a congregational meeting on August 12, 1973, Legare Walpole recommended to the congregation that the Reverend Austin Clark Wiser, aged thirty-five, then serving as the assistant minister at Tenth Presbyterian Church of Philadelphia, be elected pastor of the Johns Island Presbyterian Church. Wiser was young, originally from Los Angeles, California, and received the master of divinity from Princeton Theological Seminary in 1971. Walpole and Hills had met with him at Moncks Corner, and Wiser had visited Johns Island and the church. During his visit, he had met with two other members.

Reverend Austin Clark Wiser, minister, 1973–81. *Archives of Johns Island Presbyterian Church.*

Information about him had previously been mailed to the congregation. The recommended terms of call were an $8,500 salary, the use of the manse, $600 for manse utilities, a $600 travel allowance, $1,368 in annuity and medical insurance, four weeks' vacation and two weeks' continuing education leave. The congregation approved the call unanimously, with fifty members present and voting.

Wiser came into a time of stress and strain in the Southern Presbyterian Church. The denomination had undertaken a major restructuring of its synods and presbyteries. The redrawing and renaming of familiar boundaries and the concentration of the administrative work of the denomination under the umbrella of one large executive board in Atlanta cost a lot of money. The trust of congregations for denominational programs faltered. The winding down of the Vietnam War and the dispirited feeling after President Richard M. Nixon's resignation following the Watergate scandal contributed to the sense of unease. The effects of the civil rights legislation of the 1960s were playing out in society through the increased voting of

African Americans and the desegregation of public schools. Independent conservative movements in the denomination, like Concerned Presbyterians and the Presbyterian Lay Committee in the northern Presbyterian Church, had the effect of causing many congregations to become more independent in outlook and program support. Some congregations were separating and joining the Presbyterian Church in America.

During Wiser's pastorate, the Johns Island Presbyterian Church reflected the stresses and strains of these larger issues in society and church, but the congregation did not choose separation, and it strengthened patterns of mission in the community and abroad. Wiser and the members of the church brought the congregation into the fourth main period in the story of the people of Johns Island Presbyterian Church in the twentieth century. This period continued through the service of the next two pastors, the Reverend Ray W. Davies and the Reverend Ernest Gray.

In the early months of Wiser's ministry, several examples of deliberation and decision illustrate the larger atmosphere and the way the members of the congregation worked together. After his arrival in September 1973, the session and diaconate discussed questions of interest with the pastor and developed a program of member visitation, with a dedicated focus on finding addresses for inactive members. Wiser asked to meet with women's circles. He led a Thanksgiving service. At year's end, the statistical report showed 215 active members and a budget expenditure of $25,000. These were the largest numbers in the history of the congregation and showed that the interim planning and the work of the people with their new pastor were moving forward. In January 1974, Wiser and the session developed an organization based on commissions responsible for programmatic work, and in March, the session approved its new organization. The session minutes reflect the careful attention given to reading the Bible and praying with one another for the pastoral and program concerns before the officers.

In a competent way, the pastor and members of the Johns Island Presbyterian Church were negotiating a major change in the congregation's needs. The growth of the congregation beyond 200 members, reached when Cousar was minister, moved forward quickly. To serve the members and retain new ones, the session decided to develop program units led by lay members, through which the worship, work, pastoral care and outreach of the congregation could most effectively be administered.[163] Gradually, the Johns Island Presbyterian Church was changing from reliance on its pastor's work alone toward an approach in its leadership that encouraged greater participation and direction from lay leaders. Wiser had served with a well-known pastor in a large urban congregation. He brought skills of organization and enabled the congregation to move toward appropriate administration for a congregation of more than two hundred members in a setting that would invite further growth. Wiser and the session members collaborated to enable this development in leadership, begun when Cousar was minister, to progress.

For many years, along with its ministers, the congregation had only one continuing staff member, Mrs. John P. Limehouse, organist and choir director. After nearly thirty years of service, she resigned from her position as church organist in December 1973. In her history of the Women of the Church, Mrs. James A. Beckett noted the event and included reflections from Mrs. Limehouse as she retired.[164] The church musician said, "When I resigned as organist of the Johns Island Presbyterian Church…it seemed to me one of the hardest decisions I have had to make. It seemed I had filled a place that God had for me." She told of growing up and of her education in Georgia, until she married John Peck Limehouse and came to the island. She played music from early childhood and began in the Sunday school in 1939. After the birth of Nancy, the second daughter in the family, she was elected organist and choir director. She talked about the hand-pumped organ, requiring volunteers. Sometime the boys were not diligent and so "a new electric pump was a great improvement over the volunteer." She concluded her remarks on the occasion of her retirement by saying, "It has been my pleasure and joy to serve as organist. There were many Sundays that only with a prayer and the help of the Master that I was able to play, and not because of my feelings." These gracious words expressed the tender feeling and the deep, lifelong commitment of a member that, when shared by many others, makes a healthy church possible.

The next year, the congregation lost another prominent member. On July 2, 1974, Isabel Lofton Hills died. She was born on September 20, 1883, and was the widow of Washington Clark Hills. She became a member of the congregation in 1909. She had served in various offices of the Women of the

Church. She wrote the history of the congregation for the 250th anniversary and a short version appeared in *Sandlapper*.[165] The Women of the Church organization recognized her life and service with gratitude and expressed warm sympathy to her daughters and son. The resolution was signed by Sophie G. Wallace, Elizabeth L. Hay and Lydia C. Hay. The members of the church were gracious in their sympathy and appreciation for her dedicated service. These expressions signified a good spirit in the community.

In the meetings of the congregation, members were frank with one another about their commitments, and they took more responsibility for the decisions going forward. For example, on October 27, 1974, the slate of eight nominees for elder included two women for the first time. Julia C. Hills was named by the nominating committee; Mrs. J.S. Wallace was nominated by a member from the floor. With sixty-six members present, the members elected G.L. Buckner and B.L. Walpole to be elders from eight nominees. The next Sunday, November 3, 1974, the congregation elected G.S. Carter and Sandy Osterkamp to be deacons from a slate of twelve nominees. The congregation was breaking out of its habitual patterns of choosing its officers.

Another example of sharing thoughtful decisions came in December 1974 when the congregation met to hear a request for the clarification of benevolences to the presbytery, synod and denominational offices.[166] The pastor, Clark Wiser, advocated for supporting a world hunger relief project; Legare Walpole urged support for a mobile home ministry. The congregation designated $1,500 for the missionary couple, the Thomas Hutsons, missionaries with Wycliffe Bible translators in Brazil. Leonard Buckner urged the importance of benevolence giving. Mr. Lewis Hay moved that $2,000 out of $4,000 in the budget be designated for its fair share of benevolences given to Presbyterian work, with the addition of special offerings during the year. This proposal supported the work of the restructured Presbyterian Church (U.S.A.) and also affirmed the congregation's control over its gifts to causes of its own choosing.

The officers met for breakfast on World Communion Sunday. Aaron Leland was the cook. The session approved a devotional pamphlet for the congregation and monthly newsletters including a pastoral message. New members, the church school, youth ministry and missionary support all received renewed attention. In all of these relatively small decisions, new patterns of work emerged, and the officers led the congregation to be more responsive to the spirit in its life.

At the pastor's suggestion, the congregation decided, in November 1976, to have a committee to nominate and train nominees for service before the election for office. The congregation's concurrence simplified the nomination and election procedures, reduced the number of nominees and implied that members were more content with entrusting decisions to the pastor and the elected representatives. On January 23, 1977, the congregation elected Mr. Franklin Thomas and Mr. M. Whilden Hills to the office of elder and Mr. W.C. Hay Jr. and Mr. Ray Shokes to the office of deacon. In February 1977, Mr. Max Toole and Colonel J.C. Dove were elected deacon, and the four nominees for deacon included two women for the first time: Mrs. Daisy Leland and Mrs. Lydia Pedersen. The following year, on November 12, 1978, the members elected Mr. W.C. Hay and Mr. C.F. Davis III as elders and Mr. Marshall Hills and John Walpole as deacons. The congregation came to be comfortable with the procedures for election, and they became routine.

In February 1975, the session appointed a committee to seek the better preservation of the historic sanctuary. The church became increasingly interested in preserving the property. Through a series of carefully prepared recommendations and reports, which Mr. C.F. Davis made from February 1977 to April 1978, the congregation eventually agreed to sell about 1.4 acres of its property to St. Johns Water Company for $6,000. It was for water service for the community, not for private development. Miss Julia Hills and Mr. Clark Hills received permission from the historical committee to install a list of pastors as a memorial to their parents, Mr. and Mrs. W.C. Hills. The committee met with representatives of the National Register of Historic Places in time for recognition as a part of the United States bicentennial celebration.

Mrs. Margaret Beckett, historian of the Women of the Church, met with the National Register of Historic Places committee anticipating approval. The church allocated $4,000 for the painting of the exterior of the sanctuary. A new sign was placed at Maybank Highway and Bohicket Road. Jule Hills ordered the plaque for the recognition of the sanctuary's placement on the

National Historical Registry.[167] W.C. Hay agreed to organize workdays for the care of the cemetery under the direction of the board of deacons. The session approved guidelines for burial and ensured care of the grounds and grave sites. The appreciation for the beauty and high significance of the old sanctuary and cemetery brought the members to cherish its heritage.

The congregation continued to grow. The officers declined a request to take a public position on the Kiawah Development in February 1975. The development was moving ahead, and the minister and elders recognized the opportunity for welcoming new members as the area attracted more and more residents. In November 1975, the session approved additional nursery space. Aaron Leland, superintendent, was busy supporting the Sunday school program. The session requested the pastor to provide a short children's sermon during morning worship. The officers undertook visitation to prospective members on fourth and fifth Sundays. The people of the church came more and more to embrace the needs and gifts that were growing in their neighborhood. Members of the congregation were careful in considering the actions and changes within the Presbyterian Church. The session discussed matters related to the Presbyterian Church's adoption of a proposed *Book of Confessions*, considered denominational statements on public issues and made plans to attend the newly organized Synod of the Southeast in Columbia.[168] The session requested by letter to Mr. C.F. Davis III, chairman of the board of deacons, to make quarterly payments on Presbyterian benevolences.

Wiser asked the congregation to concur with him in his request to be released by the Charleston Presbyter from serving the congregation in 1981. His work with the people brought good experience from a large church associate position and skills for helping the Johns Island Presbyterian Church regain its momentum. His seven years of service brought continuity for the longest duration of pastoral service since Theodore Ashe Beckett left in 1945. Wiser led the church forward in developing new provisions for worship and educational ministry that invited new members. The congregation charted its own way forward in gathering increased financial resources and making benevolent contributions to ministry in the community, as well as in other lands. It contributed generously to Presbyterian benevolence causes, participated in the work of the Charleston Presbytery and was represented at the formation of the Synod of the Southeast. With the celebration of the historic sanctuary and grounds, the congregation was honoring the past while looking to the future. During Wiser's ministry, the mid-century years of shorter term pastorates ended. The next pastor, the Reverend Ray W. Davies, served eight years, from 1982 to 1990, paving the way into the last decade of the twentieth century.

Before Davies came, consultations between the session and the Charleston Presbytery Commission on Ministry offered good plans for the transition to a new leadership and brought an effective interim pastor, the Reverend Alexander M. Warren, who served from November 1981 to May 1982. During the search, the session declined to accept the request of the Rockville Presbyterian Church to share a pastor. It was judged best to have a concentration of pastoral work in the Johns Island congregation, but the session cordially invited members of the Wadmalaw Island congregation to participate in worship at Johns Island. By the end of the interim, the congregation was ready to call the new pastor, to enter with him into a well-considered strategy for mission and to agree on steps to carry it out. With the plan in place early in the ministry of Davies, the partnership of laity and new pastor provided continuity and the momentum to build on its strength and resources.

The Reverend Barry Van Deventer, stated clerk of the Charleston Presbytery, presided at the congregational meeting on November 15, 1981, which elected the nominating committee for a new pastor:

From the Session, elders M.W. Hills and C.R. McBrier
From the Deacons, Burke Lee
From the Women of the Church, Mrs. Aileen Walpole
From the Sunday School, Alvin Taylor
From the congregation at-large, Mrs. Daisy Leland and Henry J. Rast

Six months later, on May 30, 1982, Barry Van Deventer was back, the nominating committee reported, and with seventy-one members present, the congregation unanimously called the Reverend Ray Willis Davies as pastor from Peace Covenant Presbyterian Church in Key West, Florida. Davies arrived on September 21, 1982. Soon, the officers developed

Reverend Ray Willis Davies, minister, 1982–90. *Archives of Johns Island Presbyterian Church.*

a new rotational method for the elders and deacons and placed them in committees designed to lead the congregation's programs. The elders who had served through the transition and into the beginning of the new pastor's service were J.A. Beckett; W.C. Hay Sr.; M.W. Hills Sr., clerk of session; C.R. McBrier; and D.F. Thomas.

The session expressed thanks to the presbytery for the support and wrote letters of appreciation to Dr. Cousar and Mr. Warren for pastoral service during the interim.[169] To Mr. Marshall W. Hills, retiring clerk of session, the session expressed thanks for securing supply pastors and taking care of other business during the interim: "The Session of the Johns Island Presbyterian Church wishes to recognize the Christian devotion of Marshall Whilden, 'Billy' to the church, during the past few years as Clerk of Session."[170] A note of graciousness is sounded frequently by the session during these years. It marks its thanks for a variety of ministries by word and letter, and the spirit seems to carry over into the session's work.

In February 1983, the session elected C. Robert McBrier to be clerk and appointed this short set of committees of elders and members, stating clearly their program responsibilities:

> 1. *Christian Education: to include Sunday School program and literature, teacher enlistment and training, youth work, church library, retreats, camps, conferences; Members: J. Beckett, Chairman; J. Dove; all Sunday School teachers; L. Buckner; Gloria Legare; Anne Neiman; Dorothy Thomas; others can be appointed later.*
>
> 2. *Worship & Outreach: to include worship, Communion, Family Night program worship, Bible study groups meeting in homes, greeters, music, choir, pulpit supply, special services, women's work, visitation, missions, special Offerings; Members: W.C. Hay Sr., Chairman, C.R. McBrier, L. Walpole, Billy Hills, Jule Hills, Aaron & Daisy Leland, Conrad Nieman, Aileen Walpole; others can be appointed later.*[171]

In March 1989, the congregation selected six elders who had offered distinguished service and named them elders emeriti: John Dove, Henry Hay, Lewis Hay, Walter Hills, Whitemarsh Seabrook and John Wallace. This occasion was the first use of that honorary office; it was consistent with the new patterns of three-year rotations. The congregation was glad to recognize with appreciation the many years of service these men had offered.[172]

The officers took note of the new residential development of the area and planned for evangelical outreach to newcomers. In one of the few direct approaches to local government, the session called a meeting and decided to ask the Johns Island Study Committee to take up the construction of "a new roadway through Johns Island to meet the growing traffic problem."[173] The elders also wanted honest statistics of membership; thus, about seventy members were placed on the inactive roll. The list included family names of long association with the congregation.[174] Some were children of members who had left their childhood homes on Johns Island. Some had moved away. Others had drifted away. Still others left in disagreement with denominational and congregational policies and positions. The session received five new members representing three households. The growth set a trend that endured into the twenty-first century.

At the February 1983 called meeting, the session began a long-term effort to preserve and refurbish the buildings and grounds of the congregation. Also, the officers wanted to act in good faith with the spirit of placing the eighteenth-century sanctuary on the National Register of Historic Places and designating it as Site No. 114 of the American Presbyterian and Reformed Historical Sites.[175] The growing congregation needed new space. The congregation wanted to preserve and honor the contributions of many generations. Children and grandchildren representing families who had offered dedicated service for the better part of three centuries were among the members. Faithful stewardship required the officers to both change and conserve the property. The challenge in the future would be a proper balance between the gifts of God from the past for the sake of the opportunities of God for the future. This balance could grow out of the development of a strong cooperative spirit for a renewed Christian witness for a new day on the island.

At the called meeting, the session named a committee of elders and deacons who were mindful of historical preservation and asked them to study and make recommendations on improving the seating and comfort in the balcony, including access and safety. The committee began work immediately by requesting that the deacons employ a qualified restorer to repair the doors and steps on the sides for entry. Then, Legare Walpole, on behalf of the committee, solicited bids for renovation of the balcony "with consideration being given to safety, comfort, appearance, and the historical status of the church." The committee and officers met frequently in called meetings, responding to the "immediate need to improve seating conditions."[176] On May 21, 1983, Edgewood Builders, after the committee's careful consultation with Mr. David Hoffman, was authorized to begin work on the balcony.[177]

The session also asked the builder to make proposals for the renovation of the church and adjoining meeting hall. The balcony renovation began in June. It included the preservation of the remaining original benches, leaving a section of the slope of the original floor. The builder installed pews purchased from Mount Pleasant Presbyterian Church. The builder also constructed a wheelchair ramp at the rear door, with a handrail and a walkway made out of "our old English brick."[178] In September, Legare

Walpole presented the balcony committee report. "The Session expressed appreciation for how beautiful the balcony looks. It is a job very well done."[179]

During the same months the property renovations were proceeding, the northern and southern streams of the denomination were voting and bringing to conclusion in multiple meetings the reunion of the Presbyterian denominations North and South.[180] The session discussed the ins and outs of Presbyterian reunion and made a statement about the new Presbyterian Church (U.S.A.). It addressed matters of concern in the union and the behavior of some church members in relation to the issue. Some members resigned from office and membership. For these actions, the officers expressed regret. As they expressed disagreement with some aspects of the denomination's public statements on abortion and homosexuality, the elders felt that they maintained the freedom of judgment in both matters. The session expressed its readiness to give the union a chance.

Following the Plan of Union of the denomination, Mr. T.E. Pedersen accepted the appointment to identify the holders of title. The congregation moved to take title of its property as the plan permitted. In December 1983, the session called a congregational meeting to act on abstaining from the requirement that both men and women be elected elders and deacons in the newly reunited church. The elders noted that the session "is not recommending this action because it opposes having women serve as officers but it feels we should do so because we freely choose such action and not because we have to."[181] In consultation with Barry Van Deventer, stated clerk of the Charleston Presbytery, the congregation took the actions to renew the corporation, take title of the property and take the three-year exemption from the new denomination's policy of requiring the election of women officers. Six years later, in 1989, Mrs. Louise G. Davis was elected as the first woman elder in the Johns Island Presbyterian Church.

The officers put the plan for the reunited denomination to positive use. The session adopted ten covenants identifying each elder's convictions regarding the newly merged Presbyterian Church (U.S.A.).[182] A brochure for visitors and new members incorporated the covenants. The brochure listed "Our Beliefs" and gave a brief history of the congregation. The covenants also became part of the confirmation service for Sunday school teachers, particularly in accepting "the Bible as the inspired Word of God" and in requiring all teaching to be consistent with the Westminster Confession. Because the new *Book of Order* described the primary duty of the board of deacons "to minister to those who are in need, to the sick, to the friendless and to any who may be in distress," the deacons asked the session for its guidelines for these responsibilities. In January 1984, the session emphasized the deacons' responsibility for congregational and pastoral care, along with their accustomed responsibilities for ushering, financial reports and the routine maintenance of the church property. The pastor and session led the congregation to claim its own position and to take a stand within the new national Presbyterian denomination.

Davies led the congregation with strong participation in annual every-member canvass stewardship solicitations. By the end of 1982, the budget had doubled from the previous year. In 1983, James Beckett, Jule Hills, Lydia Pedersen and Dan Legare formed a strong committee for the budget and stewardship program. The good care of the property had favorable consequences in the stewardship of financial resources. In the fall of 1983, when the session heard a report on the renovations, the treasurer reported on contributions through the month of August. The amount received was more than $8,000 above the requirement for the budget, and the session felt "that every elder, deacon, and church member should praise and thank God for what He is doing with regard to the stewardship of possessions in this church."[183]

At the 1983 Thanksgiving Eve service, the improvements to the church building were dedicated with thanks to God. Each following year, the stewardship program was effective, and in October 1984, the pastor reported to the elders that the Johns Island Presbyterian Church had the highest per-capita giving of any church in the Charleston Presbytery.[184] At the end of 1984, the session approved a budget for 1985 of $118,017 and pledges of nearly $120,000. Benevolences for 1985 were budgeted for general Presbyterian support ($14,322) and other local and church related gifts, including a fund for the needy, Thornwell Orphanage, missionary support, Columbia Seminary, Presbyterian College, Montreat Anderson College, Presbyterian Outreach Foundation, Sea Island Habitat for Humanity, Rabun Gap School, Presbyterian Home in Summerville, the Gideons and Church World Relief of Hunger and Suffering. Receipts at the end of 1985 were

$187,127, and expenditures were $142,498, with $44,629 cash on hand. These reports show that the developing partnership between officers and pastor in providing inspiring leadership for the congregation yielded good financial resources for denominational and local community ministries and also sustained considerable development of the property.

The elders were also thoughtful about the way the congregation worshipped. For its own meetings, the session incorporated readings from the Bible, the *Book of Order* and the *Book of Confessions*. Time was given over to prayers for the congregation, both for the work of the officers and for pastoral concerns by name.[185] The elders addressed the need to improve the sanctuary in accord with Presbyterian and Reformed theology to acquire a Lord's table and baptismal font because "the Word and the Sacraments are central in worship." The session also addressed the conduct of services. For example, it began to use the full form of the Apostles' Creed, adding the clause often omitted, "He descended into hell."[186]

In December 1986, a new table, font and cross were approved. The session developed guidelines for weddings and funerals, revised the cemetery regulations[187] and adopted *The Singing Church*.[188] In 1988, the worship and outreach committee announced plans for Holy Week in January well in advance, with preparations for Good Friday Communion, with the "One Great Hour of Sharing" offering, and two services for Easter morning at 9:00 a.m. and 11:00 a.m.[189] The deacons assisted with the position descriptions for the church organist and managed the expansion of the choir room as the increased numbers required.[190]

Christian education for every age and youth fellowships received the support of the session and pastor. In 1982, Mr. and Mrs. Aaron Leland took on more responsibilities in the church, and they requested, after years of service, to have other leaders for the youth appointed. The session, in turn, asked them to host a meeting of the Youth Activities chairman, the Sunday school superintendent, the Christian education committee chair and others to review the past program and discuss future plans and make recommendations. Out of these plans grew a new fourth- and fifth-grade fellowship group, "the Jet Cadets," and the senior high room was expanded.[191] Midweek fellowship for adults started, and the Beckett family and others frequently welcomed them to their homes.[192] "Suppers of Eight" also gathered in homes for fellowship and hospitality.[193] The church school enrollment increased in numbers to a level it had not seen since the 1920s and '30s when the pastor gathered children from Johns and Wadmalaw by bus on Sunday afternoons. The educational program became a piece of the renewal in ministry by the congregation.

The expanded development of Seabrook and Kiawah and the attraction to new residents in the Charleston area in the 1980s offered a new opportunity to the Johns Island Presbyterian Church. However, it was the congregation's good leadership in worship, congregational care, stewardship of property and finances and Christian education that invited and consolidated its growth in membership. Already in the interim before Davies came, the congregation had welcomed new residents from near and far. In December 1981, the session sent a letter to residents of Kiawah and Seabrook, except for residents who were members of the Episcopal Church on Seabrook, to invite them to worship.[194] In March 1982, Gene Walpole was appointed to follow up with prospective members. By December 1982, the new pastor had begun commitment classes, and by February 1983, he had identified twenty-six prospective members. The officers made provisions for hospitality and welcome in worship, in fellowship and in the homes of members. When a group of twenty new members joined, they were welcomed at a congregational supper. The momentum for new members continued to build, and new family names from many new places joined the congregation.

This growth required the officers to consider the additional space needed for worship and education. In 1988, the worship and outreach committee received approval for dividing the congregation into geographical areas for better evangelism and pastoral care.[195] Naturally, the Charleston Presbytery was interested in the growth in the area. The session responded to "a rumor that the Johns Island Presbyterian Church did not want a church on Kiawah."[196] The session replied that because of their proximity, Kiawah and Seabrook were "an integral part of the ministry of the Johns island church," and with many members concurring, the congregation asked the presbytery for consultation in any plans for the development of a new congregation so that its ministry would not be jeopardized and might play a direct part in the forming of a new congregation.

The congregation also continued and reemphasized its support for world missions during the 1980s, both through the Presbyterian Church (U.S.A.) and independently. In 1982, before Davies came, the session invited Miss Angie Anderson, missionary to Zaire, to make a presentation and approve the proposal from the Women of the Church to take up a special offering for "One Great Hours of Sharing" at Easter.[197] In December 1983, the session authorized the support of the Reverend Robert and Mrs. Johnson, placed in Brazil by the Inter Varsity Christian Fellowship. In January of the same year, Dr. Edward Hay, Presbyterian missionary from Korea, spoke during the regular Presbyterian Church witness season emphasis. The congregation made its contributions personal by choosing each year to give support to several missionaries. For example, in 1989, partial support went to Mr. and Mrs. Arthur Kinsler in Korea, to Reverend and Mrs. William Warlick in Zaire and to Reverend and Mrs. Gary Waller in Mexico. For many years, since the church first offered support to John Leighton Wilson in Africa and even through poor days in the late nineteenth century, the world missionary outreach of the church was a compelling cause for the Johns Island Presbyterian congregation.

As the membership and resources grew, the congregation added to its usual support of Presbyterian causes diverse local service ministries on Johns Island and in the area. The offerings for Thornwell Orphanage, Presbyterian Homes, Presbyterian College and Columbia Theological Seminary continued. As early as 1982, the session had set up an emergency fund for local needs, served supper and breakfast at Crisis Ministry, gave to Rural Mission and Sea Island Habitat for Humanity, sponsored Red Cross bloodmobiles, visited Hermina Traye Nursing home, contributed to Mercy Ship Ministry, baked cookies for the State Corrections Institution and lent $25,000 to "needy churches." Family emergencies outside the immediate church membership from fire, illness or poverty received gifts, sometimes over extended periods of time.

Among these local ministries of outreach, none was more important than the continuing interest in the child-care center at Hebron Zion Presbyterian Church. The African American Presbyterian churches on Johns Island and Wadmalaw were founded by former members who had been slaves before the Civil War, and they continued in ministry through the years. In February 1989, the pastor attended the meeting of the Charleston Presbytery and reported to the session that the Charleston-Atlantic Presbytery had the largest black membership of any presbytery in the United States "and that the two races are working very well together."[198] The session, with the regular encouragement of the Presbyterian women's organization, gave funds to the child-care center at Hebron Zion Presbyterian Church. A hallmark of the development of the congregation in the 1980s was a conscious effort to develop support and closer ties with African American neighbors.

In the spring of 1990, Davies announced that he would retire. Preparations for the interim began. The session met to concur with and support his request to the Charleston Presbytery to allow him to retire on July 31, 1990.[199] Since he had come in September 1982, his solid leadership had brought stability and strength to the congregation and new initiatives in its programs. From the beginning of the Presbyterian Church (U.S.A.) in 1983, the congregation "gave reunion a chance" and was steady through the controversy, exercising its options under the Plan of Union for holding title to its property and electing women as officers "because we want to." The careful organization of the officers reflected due consideration to prepare for growth and strategic planning. The stewardship of the treasured property inculcated both appreciation for its historical value by placing it on the historical registers of the United States of America and the Presbyterian Church (U.S.A.) and making good renovations and adaptation for future needs. The membership and financial resources grew by careful and competent leadership of the officers. The church made notable advances in support of Christian education, pastoral care, world missions through denominational and independent agencies, local outreach and service and a growing awareness and support of African American Presbyterian neighbors. These achievements in mission gave unity and energy at a time of extraordinary opportunity for the congregation.

The last decade of the century, with the call of a new pastor, the Reverend Ernest Gray, built in significant ways on the achievements in mission by pastor and members during the 1980s. However, during his term as pastor, changes on Johns Island and in the church required a new kind of leadership and a renewed vision of the mission of Johns Island Presbyterian Church.

Reverend Ernest Gray, minister, 1991–2002. *Archives of Johns Island Presbyterian Church.*

Congregational studies have shown that when a local church moves above 350 members who are active in worship and church programs, the character of the congregation changes markedly.[200] Usually, in the smaller church one pastor and the members direct committees in organizing congregational programs. In a large church, worship, education, pastoral care, mission and the stewardship of the whole life of the church is complex. Sometimes the organization of a large church is compared to the administration of a business. This comparison with business practices does not suggest that the church *becomes* a business. A faithful congregation keeps its Christian identity and mission. On the other hand, in larger churches the pastors and members must make adjustments in expectations and organization. The large congregation requires multiple staff members under the effective supervision of the pastor, an efficient organization for specialized ministries, a strategic plan developed and regularly revised by the officers, well-designed facilities built to reflect mission priorities, substantial financial resources and a unity of purpose in mission and work. In a large congregation, the personal feel among the members cannot depend any longer on friendships and family relationships formed outside the congregation. The larger congregation must work at developing relationships that bring newcomers and old-timers together in tasks of ministry. Instead of everybody knowing everybody else, a compensating sense of community must be encouraged to grow in many groups within the congregation.

The following common interests and commitments move the mission and witness of the congregation to Jesus Christ: worship and music, care and nurture, executive leadership and planning, special volunteer services and mission, fellowship of the members, youth and children's ministry, hospitality to newcomers, administrative support and others. Successfully negotiating the change to a larger church requires both the ready acknowledgement of the gifts of long-time member families and a warm hospitality to new member families and individuals. Without acknowledging these changes and failing to develop these resources as it grows, a congregation will very likely reach a plateau or begin to decline in morale and membership.

During the 1990s, the Johns Island congregation came through the shift from a mid-sized congregation whose programs could be managed by the pastor and committees of the session into a large, complex congregation requiring specialized paid and volunteer staff members working with the minister and being reviewed and evaluated by the session through its committees. The congregation and pastor successfully managed this change in the size and nature of the congregation, and the Johns Island Presbyterian

Church had gained strong momentum by the time Ernest Gray retired as minister, after eleven years of service, on December 29, 2002.

Signs of change in the Johns Island area appeared all around. In his reports to the session, Gray accounted for change by reminding the officers that Johns Island was becoming suburban. The city limits of Charleston came to Angel Oak. "The Luxurious Lowcountry" kept on attracting many new residents.[201] The Sea Islands continued to leave behind traditional rural economy, while real estate and services generated new wealth. African American residents continued to move away, while Hispanic and other immigrants brought new diversity to the population. The points of change were visible in several aspects of the church's life:

1) The growing congregation began to need two worship services on Sunday mornings. An early service began on an experimental basis and later became permanent.

2) The plan to unite the work of elders and deacons in one body on the session lasted, and the placement of elders with other gifted members for specific work on committees and their rotation in three-year cycles became the norm.

3) Educational ministries of the congregation increased and became more diverse. The session called a director of youth ministry who developed a cooperative youth fellowship with Rockville Presbyterian and St. Johns Episcopal Church. A full-time director of Christian education was called.

4) The stewardship of the buildings led the congregation to a well-planned, financed and beautifully executed restoration of the eighteenth-century sanctuary and refurbishing of the fellowship hall.

5) The budget increased every year. The pastor began making thorough annual reports to the session during the stewardship season in 1994 to mark the growth in financial resources and membership. Statistical reporting to the presbytery became an opportunity for strategic information and planning.

6) The congregation's long support of global missions grew stronger and became directed toward more emphasis on Presbyterian mission fields. With the arrival of "Luxurious Lowcountry" living, local poverty and incoming immigrants, particularly Hispanic immigrants, presented new opportunities and demands for service. The financial needs of Hebron Zion Presbyterian

Church were more often a matter of concern, and Johns Island Presbyterian offered support to its sister African American congregation.

These six points of change tell the story of how the Johns Island Presbyterian Church moved from the twentieth century into the twenty-first. Comments on these points, with selected illustrations, make up the story of the ministry of Johns Island Presbyterian Church in the last decade of the twentieth century.

Worship

It was becoming clear that the church needed another regular opportunity for worship to supplement the traditional Sunday morning service. On a trial basis, in June 1992 the session approved an early worship service on Sunday mornings, but the services were discontinued after October 25, 1992. Meanwhile, the congregation developed new worship practices. In April 1993, the congregation began to celebrate Scottish Heritage Sunday with some brave men wearing kilts. Tartans hung, bagpipes played and dinner on the grounds followed. In its first year, the festival celebrated completion of part of the restoration of the sanctuary; it is now an annual spring event. In February 1994, the session approved a worship service on Kiawah for Easter. The following year, an Easter Service at 8:30 a.m. on Easter morning gathered the congregation in the sanctuary.[202] At the same time, the church nursery was expanding, and a position description for a nursery worker received approval.[203]

A full-time nursery attendant, Lela Hazel, provided child care for services and church activities, and in the spring of 1996, the session employed another nursery attendant. At the end of the summer of 1996, the session recognized Gail Hay for her work in directing the nursery, and good attendance at the nine o'clock morning services from June through Labor Day confirmed the continuing need for offering members the flexibility of choosing the hour.[204] Beginning on March 2, 1997, two Sunday morning worship services were established, with monthly Communion at 9:00 a.m. and quarterly at 11:00 a.m. In October 1999, the session approved the purchase of video broadcast equipment at a cost of $8,000 to accommodate, by closed circuit, the overflow expected at the Christmas Eve service. An anonymous donor contributed $4,000 toward its purchase.

In December 1999, the worship committee set a limit for sanctuary seating of 230 persons and directed overflow to the fellowship hall. In April 2000, Rod James, Robert Lanier, Mary Hills and Jay Frickman were appointed to prepare a statement that was to "help the Session and Congregation understand the future Staffing/Building space needs."[205] These changes to accommodate growing attendance at worship—including the new celebration of Communion and Scottish heritage, additional choir and music leadership, flexibility of worship spaces and a plan for enlargement of the building—are the first indicator of the new requirements of the congregation in the 1990s.

Congregational Care

Throughout Gray's ministry, the session was attentive to the older generation, which had served the congregation for many years. It regularly approved older members for admission to the Presbyterian Home in Summerville. Other special events too numerous to mention—birthdays, anniversaries, retirements, long service, etc.—prompted the session to recognize older members and their families, even while many newcomers were becoming a part of the worship and work of the congregation. Some long-term members who had fallen by the wayside received visits and were entered back on the active roll. Wedding guidelines were approved to establish good procedures for increasing requests for marriage services. New members and old accepted the stated guidelines for church use, and Nancy Carter served as the first wedding director. The wedding plans of the Roddey family for their daughter received approval according to the guidelines about the time they moved to Kiawah and joined the church. Following the same procedure, the session welcomed the marriage of a granddaughter of the James Beckett family who had been in the church for generations.

Every year, older members were passing away, and in 1994, the congregation lost T.A. Beckett III, Lewis H. Hay Jr., Lewis W. Gantt, Roberta Meyer, Whitemarsh Seabrook and John Reese. An older generation was passing away, calling for new leaders. Regular visits to deliver worship service tapes to shut-in members became a regular practice. In October 1998, Mary Dove expressed to Norma Beckett and Ruth McIver during their visit that the ministry meant a great deal to her and her husband.[206] Women and men visited homebound members and sent cards. Attention to cordial welcome for new members was regular. In August 2000, the session received a letter of thanks from the family of Lydia Hay, who passed away after many years of prominent service to Women of the Church as treasurer and in many other roles in the congregation. Another letter came when Julia Hills died in October 2000, and another arrived from the family of Thomas Legare in November 2000.

The session also supported the staff members when trouble came. When Mrs. Gray, mother of the pastor, died, the session recorded that the congregation "extended our love, special thoughts, and prayer to Ernie, Peggy, and the family."[207] In June 2001, the session gave the music director, Linda Sue Horres, full salary while she was absent recovering from an automobile accident, and in December, it supported the administrative assistant, Barbara Burger, for her surgery sick leave. The pastor regularly took Communion to the homebound. For example, Elder Ellis Hay assisted Gray in taking the sacrament to John and Nancy McKee at their home in October 2002. In November 2003, a *Book of Remembrances* for recording memorials given to the church was approved to mark the many expressions of Christian sympathy and support. The minister and elders had an instinct for providing good pastoral care for older and new members. Rapid change and the passing of older members brought stresses to the congregation, but good care assured members of God's care and healing.

Growth of Membership and Session Reorganization

In the early weeks of his coming, Gray gave attention to the opportunity for growth in membership. Thirty members joined between January and June, and in August 1994, Gray reported 430 active members. He attributed the increase, in part, to hospitality and fellowship gatherings in homes. In his 1994 fall report, Gray reported on the significant increases in the population of Seabrook, Kiawah and the Andell development. At his recommendation, the session devoted regular attention to strategic planning for land use.

Reorganization for growth also required new administrative procedures and new people to do accustomed tasks. In December 1994, the session asked Jim McCallister to devise a new description of the treasurer's position and to automate the records. The session recognized Lydia Pedersen, treasurer, and offered thanks to Ruth Leasure, accountant. In July 1995, the session led the congregation to honor Miss Julia Hills for service as clerk of the congregation for thirty-five years. The quality and care of her minutes gave fine form to the official records of the congregation. Daisy Leland agreed to select a gift and plan its presentation. The new focus on personnel policies and administration received approval from the congregation at a meeting in December 1996, when Barry Van Deventer from the office of the Charleston Presbytery presided.

Notice was given to the new relocation and expansion of the choir space, the expansion of the nursery for morning worship and the new descriptions for the work of administrative assistant and custodian. A 5 percent increase in the pastor's salary received congregational approval. The adding of ministries created greater need for services from employed staff, and at mid-year 1996 the session gave salary increases to Karen Groom, custodian, and Mattie Nielsen, church secretary. This consideration of staff salaries continued through the years of Gray's ministry. In October 1996, the officers established the personnel committee with two elders and three at-large members. The growing staff and responsibilities required good business practices in employment, evaluation and compensation. The personnel policies included a written position description and interviews for all prospective employees.[208] With a new computer system and the donation of equipment, the church developed a website (ww.jipc.org) and online service.[209]

The rotation of the elders on the session brought regular attention to its organization, and the congregation was obliged to make nominations and elect officers every year. This procedure had the advantage of bringing to mind the continuing work of the governing body, and it added new names, along with the election of former elders after a rest of at least one year. Accountability and focus on the programs came in part through the appointment of capable congregation members for specific roles. For example, Robert F. Lanier Jr. became treasurer. When he rotated off the session, he resigned in June 2002, and the new treasurer, Tom Burke, was introduced to the session at the same meeting.[210] Likewise, regular rotation and review required attention to a variety of services offered by members of the congregation. For example, Patty Anderson was appointed to organize a children's church, Trudy Reeder became chairperson for the nurseries and a council for the ecumenical youth fellowships supported the work of the youth director.

The annual reports confirmed that the officers and congregation came to understand the church in a new way. Johns Island Presbyterian Church had become "a suburban congregation," and with new worship schedules, education and fellowships, hospitality to newcomers and missions both globally and locally, the work of the congregation required new staff, resources for planned giving, a building endowment, wills emphasis, investment management and the development of the officers in organization and training.[211]

Education for Children, Youth and Adults

Throughout its history, the pastors and elders offered opportunities for teaching the Bible and gathering the young and adult members for Christian nurture in classes. Even when the session minutes are spare, the appointment of a Sunday school superintendent is noted. During Gray's ministry, the session called qualified persons to serve on the church staff to support the program of Christian education. In 1994, Carolyn Slay became Christian education director. She brought continuing focus and new energy for children and youth. She planned a fall congregational retreat with presentations on Thornwell Children's Home, Samaritan's Purse and World Medical Missions. In September, she reported to the session on the organization of fellowship groups for children and youth from first grade through high school.

In March 1995, the Christian education committee asked permission for a Wednesday afternoon program for elementary-age children with a meal and study. The session approved a trial period for a Logos program. In April, a good report on the strong response to the program came to the session, and after the June event, it gained the accolade of "total success."[212] In

September 1995, Mrs. Zoe Anne Cagle was called to organize a joint youth fellowship for Rockville, Johns Island and St. Johns Episcopal Churches on a year trial.

In June 1998, the session approved the employment of a Christian educator to develop plans for the growing numbers of young people moving into new affordable housing developments in the area, and in August, Mrs. Deborah K. Neal came as director of Christian education and served until June 1999.[213] In the fall, the Christian education committee reported on continuing plans for Logos youth ministry, and in December, Mrs. Alexis Morris received warm welcome as the new director of Christian education. The session noted in February 2000, "Alexis is doing a great job, and remember, she is for adults too!" She trained Presbyterian Youth Connection teachers, prepared worship aids for children in morning worship, requested approval of a new curriculum and arranged for the annual summer vacation Bible school. She became a certified associate church educator through the training program offered by the Presbyterian Church (U.S.A.). The Rockville Presbyterian Church youth again began meeting with the Johns Island fellowships on Sunday evenings, and their children joined the Logos program on Wednesdays. In November 2001, a confirmation class for older youth brought Brittany Branyon and Lindsay Severson into the membership.[214]

In November 2001, the session expressed congratulations to Milton and Alexis Morris on the birth of their son, Ivan Edward Morris, and granted his mother two months maternity leave with full pay.[215] In cooperation with the presbytery in the summers of 2000 through 2003, the session approved a satellite program, granting permission to the staff of Camp Bethelwoods to hold a weeklong program in July for thirty-six youths from the area. New elder training was included in the reports on the Christian education program, and in 2002, two new adult classes began.[216]

Educational ministry for children, youth and adults required continuing attention, regular planning and careful recruitment and support of capable new staff members. It was essential for its growth and developing strength that the congregation developed new leadership for the nurture of children, youth and adults. The session and members embraced a strong educational program.

The Twentieth Century

Restoration of Sanctuary and Strategic Planning

In April 1992, the officers consulted with a restoration specialist. Scrubbing and painting of the clapboard exterior commenced. Landscaping still needed to catch up from Hurricane Hugo destruction.[217] Walpole and Legare donated sod, Ted and Norma Beckett gave azaleas and volunteers planted shrubbery. The session took out an advertisement in the Yellow Pages calling newcomers to the "oldest Presbyterian structure in continuous use" in the United States. Later, the claim would have to say "wooden frame structure," but the point about the unique history of the congregation was clear. In 1993, Billy Hills reported for the restoration effort on the completed refurbishment of the pews, and in May, the congregation celebrated with dinner on the grounds after worship. The "old Communion table" was marked with a plaque and replaced the modern one. The long pine table fit with the refurbished sanctuary.

In 1994, the session entered negotiations for the purchase of the Sosnowski property adjacent to the church. In the spring of the same year, Gray reported to the session that increasing membership would lead to a year-end number "approaching four hundred."[218] In March 1995, the planners stated that they were considering ways and means for land use for the following ten years and a potential church membership of eight hundred.[219] As partial fruit of the planning, by April 1995, the move of the choir loft to the balcony, the expansion of seating toward the front and the restoration of the pulpit area were under way according to carefully approved architectural design.[220] The session authorized new hymnbooks, and in June, by a special order, it approved a recital by Linda Sue Horres on a new organ. In July, the strategic planning committee received approval for funding to support its fees payable to Mr. Opperman and received a bid by Total Restoration Company for the sanctuary restoration. The fall congregational retreat heard a report on the plans, including consideration of "Proposed Land Usage." Later, in 1995, the pastor's call was changed to allow him to vacate the manse and receive a housing allowance for the purchase of a house for his family.

The planning continued, with regular reports to the session and the congregation. In support of the planning and funding for the property, the corporation elected new officers in 1996: president, Legare Walpole; vice-president, Billy Hay; clerk, James Beckett; and treasurer, Jim McCallister. In 1996, the General Endowment Fund Council was created with officers elected for three-year terms; Ellis Hay, Roger McLaughlin, Daisy Leland, Gordon Fuqua and Donald Ruff made up the first committee. Ruff took charge of an educational effort for the fund in the congregation. The corporation tended to its work and annually renewed its officers. Although it was intent on local outreach and mission and cooperative with other congregations, the session nevertheless refused the request of Sea Island Habitat for the sale of some of its forty acres of property for Habitat home sites, and it denied a request from the Catholic Church to purchase property for the development of its new building.[221]

In October 1997, the long-range planning committee reported on the increasing population on the islands and the real need for professional assistance in planning for the facilities and "the use of the entire plot of property."[222] The committee concluded that it was reasonable to expect the congregation to reach seven to eight hundred members in the next ten years. In January 1998, the long-range planning committee held bimonthly small group meetings with about twenty members in the church conference room on Sunday mornings. In September 1999, the session referred to the planning committee a report on a survey of the congregation by Rod and Ruth Ann James on a proposal to build a columbarium in the church cemetery.[223] The officers appointed a new cemetery committee: Chairman Bill Hay, with Elders Ellis Hay, Leonard Buckner and Daisy Leland. In August 2002, the regulations were revised to prohibit pets from burial and to have markers for the ashes that were scattered.

In April 2000, Rod James, Robert Lanier, Mary Hills and Jay Frickman were appointed to prepare a statement that was to "help the Session and Congregation understand the future Staffing/Building space needs." Their "Statement of Ministry for the Johns Island Presbyterian Church" was approved in May 2000. The pastor wrote the summary. After a preamble on the understanding of the ministry of the church, the statement offers guidelines for the development of the property to provide for the future ministry of the congregation to the Johns Island community. In three points the statement recommends:

1) maintaining and preserving the present sanctuary.

2) building a family life center for "a pleasant, safe environment adequate for teaching and learning and inviting for fellowship and recreation."

3) appointing a building committee with responsibilities for engaging an architect, presenting plans by October 2000, and, when the addition is completed, the demolition of the present fellowship hall.[224]

The preamble reads:

> *This church understands itself to be an on-going representation of the body of our Lord Jesus Christ. Our first duty is to worship our God who is represented as Father, Son and Holy Spirit. We worship in praise and with thanksgiving. Sustained and encouraged by our worship our ministry leads us to study God's Word, teach our children and example for them a godly way of living. Our goal is to let each person know they matter to God, by showing them they matter to us, in order that they may let others matter to them. In this spirit of caring we seek to live out our love for God in service to each other, the greater community and world. We invite all to join in the joy of our faith and in celebration of God's love.*

In May 1999, W.H. "Billy" Hills volunteered to conduct historical tours of the church building. A number of people agreed to help. A sign indicated the hours, and the session approved having a box in the back of the sanctuary for those visitors who wanted to make contributions. Hills presented a video of his historic tours, which was applauded by the elders and received with thanks as "quite a treasure" by the minister.[225]

In the decade of the 1990s, the congregation responded to the growing population of the Johns Island area by developing and regularly revising a strategic plan for its property and programs. It resolved to honor the heritage of the sanctuary and the land. Excellent renovation and restoration of the old sanctuary building preserved its character in accord with the requirements of its placement on the National Register of Historic Places and its designation as a Presbyterian and Reformed Historical Site. To support new church programs, the congregation made

Communion table, baptismal font and pulpit. The careful renovation in the 1990s renewed the beauty and preserved the usefulness of the historic sanctuary. *Photograph by Katharine Bair.*

appropriate adaptations of the newer buildings and laid plans for further construction. These extraordinary plans and accomplishments signaled the congregation's growing support for a new day in the ministry of Johns Island Presbyterian Church.

Stewardship of Financial Resources

Growing in membership and expanding in ministries cost a lot of money, and during the 1990s the officers sought a new commitment to the stewardship of financial resources. The support did not always come as needed. For example, in August 1993, budgeted funds for operating expenses fell short, and pew refinishing was sponsored by individual pledges.[226] However, in every year of the decade, the congregation supported increased budgets. In December 1993, after the restoration of the pews left a surplus, the session heard that the proposed 1994 budget of $189,090 was within $2,000 pledged in support.[227] Consistent with new demands on church staff, the funds for Christian education increased, and a 5 percent staff salary raise became a part of the 1995 budget recommendation.

At the end of 1996, membership had risen by 25 new members to 432, and the receipts for the budget were $290,857, a new high mark. In 1997, an automated system of accounting, also developed for the session by McCallister, made regular reports to the officers and congregation. A capital expenditure review separate from regular budgeting and an approval procedure for expenses became standard policies. Four Sundays a year, the session brought the endowment fund to the attention of the congregation. In March 1997, the audit report of the Charleston Presbytery commended the session on the excellent quality of its records.[228] Throughout the decade, the officers gave careful attention to the program of financial stewardship. An expanding and complex church program required more money. Better reporting helped build confidence in the session. Stewardship education generated enthusiasm among the members for the property improvements, the support of the church staff and increasing commitment to the mission of the church both globally and in the neighborhood.

Global and Local Missions

The congregation grew in its awareness and support of the ministry of the church outward into the world, both through international and local mission commitments. The congregation kept emphasizing and supporting world missions, following the suggested witness season of the Presbyterian denomination. For example, in 1993, Dr. Birch Rambo, medical missionary to Zaire (now the Democratic Republic of the Congo), spoke to the congregation, and with representatives from the congregation he participated in a medical mission fair at the Medical University of South Carolina on January 26–27, 1993. The support of Wycliffe Bible translators was terminated in favor of a Presbyterian global mission. Later in October, the Reverend and Mrs. Art Kinsler visited while on furlough from Korea. Beginning in 1994, Dr. and Mrs. John Fowler, serving in Turkey, received support. Dr. Don Mullen spoke at the Sunday morning services in September 1997 during the witness season emphasis.

The session responded to missionaries it supported in Japan, Reverend and Mrs. Vincent Stubbs, to help raise funds to start Nara Reformed Church.

The session committed $1,000 to the effort and promised to consider more in the budget for 1998. Johns Island increased in yearly budgeted funds for the partial support of several selected missionaries abroad. In April 1999, the budget for the total amount was $12,200, and when the mission and outreach committee heard that two of its supported missions were fully funded, the extra was allocated to Mr. and Mrs. Juan Kaer in Argentina. In 2001, the congregation began sponsoring the Reverend Mark S. Adams, co-director of *Frontera de Cristo* in Douglas, Arizona, part of the Presbyterian Border Ministry.[229] In October 2000, the session, at the recommendation of Elder Tom Ferguson, paid expenses for two church members to participate in a March 2003 mission to Haiti.

To set reasonable limits on requests to the congregation and to cooperate with denominational programs, the outreach and mission committee had the session approve five special offerings a year: One Great Hour of Sharing for World Relief at Easter, Presbyterian Homes of South Carolina at Mother's Day, witness season offering for Global Mission, Thornwell Home and School at Thanksgiving and the Joy Gift Offering at Christmas.[230] World mission came home in a vivid way. Elder Rick Foster, MD, and his daughter, Ashlee, joined a large group of young people from across the nation in an independent mission project to build a hospital and to offer medical services in the Dominican Republic.[231] In another example of the local mission connecting with the global mission, a Johns Island resident, Mrs. Lisa Santiago, went to El Salvador on a medical mission trip, accompanying cardiologists and other physicians. She spoke at the family night supper in October 1997 about the mission.

Young people became a regular part of the mission work of the congregation. The combined youth groups of Johns Island, Rockville and St. Johns Episcopal Churches participated with Jeannie Koenig in the Hispanic Ministry and developed a mission statement.[232] In February 2000, they made cookies for the Kairos Mission, and Ed and Ethel Wenrich met with the junior and senior highs to tell them about missionary support. At Christmas, youth prepared a dinner for the congregation with proceeds to sponsor local families with youth. It was a success, and young people suggested by Rural Mission and Sea Island Habitat for Humanity came for the Adopt-a-Family party in December 2000.[233] In 2001, young people began participating in the "Souper Bowl" program and contributed their collection of $1,429 to the Our Lady of Mercy assistance program and Bread of Life Food Ministry.

In 1992, Jeannie Koenig, a member of Westminster Presbyterian Church in Charleston, requested permission to use the fellowship hall for teaching English to immigrants; under her leadership, this ministry became an extraordinary program of assistance, hospitality and service. Soon, annual Hispanic Christmas parties were being organized, and a comprehensive ministry by volunteers offered tutorials, assistance and clothing to migrant farm workers and permanent residents. The ministry continued, and in 1997 the session approved the use of the fellowship hall for worship services, saying, "Most of the work has been accomplished by one truly dedicated person, Jeannie Koenig."[234] A year later, the session heard another report and listed an extraordinary number of services to the growing Hispanic community of migrant laborers and residents. The services included education, food, clothing, worship, pastoral care for marriages and funerals, financial assistance and other means of hospitality for these new neighbors outside the membership of the congregation but within the care and concern of the members.[235] In November 1998, a building was found for the Hispanic ministry, and the session approved funds for the ministry in a new location.

The congregation engaged in a broad range of volunteer ministries and offered financial assistance for crisis ministry and relief of personal hardships in the community. The congregation's intention and resources directed toward local mission attracted loyal attention from members. In a notable example, in November 1997, a member designated a gift of $61,570 to be divided among the local ministries of the congregation in the Johns Island neighborhood, including substantial amounts for the John and Mattie Washington Preschool of the Hebron Zion Presbyterian Church; the Charleston Interfaith Crisis Ministry, through Charleston Atlantic Presbytery; Thornwell Home; the Johns Island Presbyterian Church Hispanic Ministry; and to the Pastor's Discretionary Benevolence Fund. The congregation provided housing for out-of-town volunteers working with Sea Island Habitat for Humanity. In the local community, volunteers continued to serve meals at Crisis Assistance Ministry in Charleston. Felix Nepveux and Ethel Wenrich played for the Hermina Traye Nursing Home gatherings. Dr. Nepveux thanked the session for large-print songbooks supplied for this ministry.

Month after month, local benevolence funds were given to various persons. In 1997, the session provided for a church member who needed medicine, and a member responded to the request of a handicapped person for assistance with financial planning. A family whose home was burned was given assistance, and a session member made a personal contribution to the church, designated for the family.[236] In February 1998, the outreach and mission chairman reported meeting with the Edisto Island Presbyterian Church and began a partnership in a Mobile Dental Unit. The report said, "This is a very vital addition to our serious health assistance to the needy black and Hispanic farm community."[237] An offering was approved for a family whose home was struck by a tornado.[238]

In April 1995, the session heard that the senior citizens' organization at Hebron Zion Presbyterian Church needed support and approved a gift. In October, another gift was given. The children's ministry in that congregation also received support; in April 1997, the John and Mattie Washington Preschool was given $1,500. Continuing assistance was offered to the sister congregation. In 2000, Hebron Zion Presbyterian Church called the Reverend Henry Rivers as pastor, and Ernest Gray participated in the installation service.[239]

Regular letters of thanks came to the session for the remarkable ministries outside the congregation from: Samaritans Purse, Theological Education Fund of the Presbyterian Church (U.S.A.); Our Lady of Mercy Catholic Church; Siloam Eye Hospital; Thornwell Home and School; Near East School of Theology in Lebanon; Rabun Gap School in Georgia; the Medical Benevolence Foundation; and a local family who received aid.[240] These letters showed that part of the development of the new quality of ministry and service during the 1990s and beyond was a vigorous and strengthened commitment of the people of Johns Island Presbyterian Church to serving others in the name of Jesus Christ at home and abroad.

Looking back over these six areas in the program during the ministry of Ernest Gray, we can see a remarkable change in the worship and work of the congregation. These points of emphasis did not begin during the last decade of the twentieth century. The development in all of them grew from roots established over many generations. The worship in the treasured sanctuary and congregational care, the attention to education and youth ministry, the stewardship of funds in good times and in bad, the organization and management of the congregation through Presbyterian Church order and the mission of the people in world and local ministries had been faithfully conducted for many years. However, the complexity and demands of carrying on these ministries in a vital way in the last decade of the twentieth century required new provisions. The congregation enlarged and reorganized its officers and program; employed, supported and evaluated new staff members; and developed written strategic plans and revised them regularly. Through these last years in the twentieth century and into the twenty-first, the records of the Johns Island Presbyterian Church show a dedication to the Christian faith, a harmony in carrying out its mission and a spirit of fellowship and service in its life.

In August 2002, Dr. Ernest Gray announced his proposed retirement after eleven years as pastor of Johns Island Presbyterian Church. "With great regret the Session as a body approved his request."[241] On Sunday, December 29, 2002, the congregation concurred with the pastor and the recommendation of the session so that he might be honorably retired.[242] In September, he outlined the procedure for obtaining an interim minister. Elders Tom Ferguson, Ellis Hay, Mary Hills, Rod James and Aileen Walpole were appointed to an ad hoc committee to interview and recommend to the session an interim pastor. The session approved the Reverend Barry Van Deventer to become the interim minister on February 1, 2003. "He will be available 2 Sundays in January and his son will preach 1 Sunday in January."[243] On January 14, 2003, Mr. Ferguson presented the "Interim Pastor Agreement" to the session, which Mr. Van Deventer accepted.

Mary Hills was elected moderator of the session on January 14, 2003. The session appointed members to the new pastor-nominating committee: Alene Bass, Mary Bird Ferguson, Aileen Walpole and Coy Foster as alternate. The congregation elected at-large members on March 2, 2003: Guy Leonard Buckner, Jim McCallister, Jim Nicholson and Bennie Slay. On October 14, 2003, Jim McCallister presented to the session the "Proposed Terms of Call" for the Reverend Jonathan Van Deventer, associate pastor at First Presbyterian Church in Aiken, South Carolina. The session unanimously approved the recommendation, and on November 2, 2003, the congregation issued a call to the new pastor. He was installed on Sunday, December 7, 2003, at 3:30 p.m. His pastoral leadership continues today.

Appendix

RULING ELDERS OF JOHNS ISLAND PRESBYTERIAN CHURCH

Kinsey Burden, before 1855
James Legare, before 1855
Thomas Legare, before 1855
J.A. Fripp, 1855–1870
D.J. Townsend, MD, 1856–1875
Hugh Wilson Jr., 1859–1861
W.S. Whaley, MD, 1859–1885
J.L. Stevens, 1870–1874
J.B.L. Walpole, 1870–1893
F.Y. Legare Sr., 1884–1905
J.C.W. Legare, 1895–1906
H.C. Mühler, 1904–1918
G.W. Hills, 1907–1915
E.M. Seabrook, 1907–1926
J.L. Seabrook, 1913–1936
T.S. Legare, 1915–1927
L.H. Hay Sr., 1919–1940
T.A. Beckett Sr., 1919–1947
J.B. Walpole, 1926–1929
E.G. Hay, 1929–1936
K.W. Leland, 1929–1980

G. Walter Hills, 1936–1950

W.C. Hills, 1936–1964

D.E. Hay, 1944–1968

E.V. Legare, 1944–1969

L.H. Hay Jr., 1950–1989, elder emeritus

J.S. Wallace, 1950–1989, elder emeritus

J.A. Beckett, 1967–1980, 1990–1992, 1992–1994

B.L. Walpole Sr., 1968

W. F. Schwuchow, 1968, 1983

W.C. Hay, 1968–1978, 1988–1990

Guy L. Buckner, 1968–1974, 1989–1990, 1991–1993

Aaron W. Leland, 1972–1984, 1986

B.L. Walpole Jr., 1974–1976, 1983–1985, 1995–1997

D. Franklin Thomas, 1977

M. Whilden Hills Sr., 1977, 1986–1988, 1997–1999

Bennie Slay, 1978, 1991–1993

C.F. Davis III, 1978, 1988–1990

C. Robert McBrier, 1980

Louise Grimball Davis, 1989–1991

Mack Watson, 1990–1991

Edward Turner, 1984–1986

Hubert A. Osterkamp, 1984–1986

Grayson Carter, 1985–1987

William Gamble, 1985–1987

John Dove, 1983–1985, 1989, elder emeritus

H.M. Hay, 1989, elder emeritus

W.A. Hills, 1989, elder emeritus

W.B. Seabrook, 1989, elder emeritus

Ed Wenrich, 1990–1992

Robert Harding, 1990–1992

James Hammersmith, 1990–1992, 1994–1996, 2005

Ralph Stevens, 1991–1993

Ruth McIver, 1991–1993, 1998–2000

Lydia Pedersen, 1990–1992, 1997–1999, 2009–2011

C.O. Grooms Jr., 1991–1993, 1997–1999, 2009–2011

Ruling Elders of Johns Island Presbyterian Church

Doris Fowler, 1992–1994

James McCallister, 1992–1994

John Branyon Jr., 1992–1994

Dorothy Frick, 1992–1994

Leonard Buckner, 1993–1995

Felix Nepveux, 1993–1995

Milton Morgan, 1993–1995, 1998–2000

Norma Beckett, 1993–1995, 1999–2001

Grayson Carter, 1994–1996

Mack Watson, 1994–1996

Daisy Barron Leland, 1994–1996, 2003–2005

Donald Ruff, 1995–1997

Nancy Stevens, 1995–1997

Nancy Anne Ritchie, 1995–1997, 2002–2004

Gordon Fuqua, 1996–1998

Janie Gantt, 1996–1998

William C. Hay Jr., 1996–1998

Rick Foster, 1996–1998, 2009–2011

James C. Nicholson, 1997–1999

Mattie Nielsen, 1997–1999

Barbara Hubbeling, 1998–2000

Robert Lanier, 1998–2000

Joe Fortune, 1999–2001

Tom Koenig, 1999–2001

Trudy Hay Reeder, 1999–2001

Tom Ferguson, 2000–2002

Jay Frickman, 2000–2002

Mary Gervais Hills, 2000–2002

Rodney James, 2000–2002

Gail Fortune, 2001–2003

Ellis Hay, 2001–2003

Menry Meise, 2001–2003

Aileen Samford Walpole, 2001–2003

Alene Bass, 2002–2003

Coy Foster, 2002–2004

Anne Kennan, 2002–2004
Harvey Sewell, 2002–2004
Lowell Bernard, 2003–2005
Tom Burke, 2003–2005
Mary Bird Ferguson, 2003–2005
David Anderson, 2004–2006
Sandra Buckner Branyon, 2004–2006
Laura Sewell, 2004–2006
Loren Van Oordt, 2004–2006
Aileen Walpole Halford, 2005–2007
Jan Litton, 2005–2007, 2008–2010

Notes

Preface

1. Clarke, *Our Southern Zion*.

Part I

2. Ahlstrom, *Religious History*, 84–92.
3. Betts, *South Carolina Methodism*, 11–16.
4. Edgar, *South Carolina*, 1–2.
5. Ibid., 43.
6. Ibid., 46–50.
7. Wallace, *South Carolina*, 28, 30, 32–33. Edgar, *South Carolina*, 84–85.
8. Wallace, *South Carolina*, 38, 197.
9. Clarke, *Our Southern Zion*, 29–32, 39–42.
10. Ibid., 32. See also Clarke, *Wreslin' Jacob* and *Dwelling Place*.
11. Howe, *History*, I, 140.
12. Fludd, *Biographical Sketches*, 32.
13. Ibid., 32. See also Howe, *History*, I, 160.
14. Howe, *History*, I, 165.
15. Ibid., 146, 170.

16. Ibid., I, 170.

17. Reprinted in Carroll, *Historical Collections*.

18. Howe, *History*, I, 191.

19. Ibid., 191.

20. "An Early Historical Account," in Smith, *Stono*, 33–34.

21. Howe, *History*, I, 227.

22. Edgar, *South Carolina*, 100, 102–07.

23. Quoted in Howe, *History*, I, 207.

24. Clarke, *Our Southern Zion*, 84–88.

25. Fludd, *Biographical Sketches*, 65–70. See also Howe, *History*, I, 396.

26. *South Carolina Gazette*, August 15, 1753, quoted in Howe, *History*, I, 278.

27. Howe, *History*, I, 271.

28. Ibid., 321.

29. Ibid.

PART II

30. Clarke, *Our Southern Zion*, 36–38.

31. Edgar, *South Carolina*, 330–38.

32. Clarke, *Our Southern Zion*, 105–07.

33. Howe, *History*, I, 573.

34. Ibid., II, 61–62.

35. Clarkson Correspondence, December 29, 1997; January 18, 1998.

36. Howe, *History*, II, 230.

37. Brewster Correspondence.

38. His gravestone gives the date as September 11, 1814, but a letter from Anson Brewster to his wife tells of his visits to the grave in November 1813. Brewster Correspondence, December 4, 1813.

39. Brewster Correspondence, December 4, 1813.

40. Howe, *History*, II, 230–31.

41. Swinton Family Society, "Charts."

42. Hills and McIver, *Johns Island Presbyterian*, 63–64.

43. Howe, *History*, II, 317.

44. Ruchames, *House Divided*, 301, note 3.

45. The memorial in the sanctuary says "twenty years." It is incorrect. Compare to Hills and McIver, *Johns Island Presbyterian*, 133.
46. Howe, *History*, II, 618. Howe's calculations of dates are not correct here. See page 331.
47. Hills and McIver, *Johns Island Presbyterian*, 63, G4.
48. Porcher and Fick, *Story of Seas Island Cotton*, 341–54.
49. Haynie, *Images of America*, 18–19; Jordan and Stringfellow, *Place Called St. John's*, 238–40.
50. Porcher and Fick, *Sea Island Cotton*, 315.
51. Howe, *History*, II, 332. See also Jordan and Stringfellow, *Place Called St. John's*, 130–31. Compare to Hills and McIver, *Johns Island Presbyterian*, 28.
52. See "Six Ways to Compute the Relative Value of a U.S. Dollar Amount, 1774 to Present," Measuring Worth, http://www.measuringworth.com/calculators/uscompare (accessed December 2009).
53. M. Hills, *Johns Island Presbyterian*, 2–3.
54. Jones, *Catechism*; Clarke, *Wrestlin' Jacob*, 49–52; Clarke, *Our Southern Zion*, 131–34.
55. Edgar, *South Carolina*, 328–30; Clarke, *Our Southern Zion*, 122–30.
56. Clarke, *Our Southern Zion*, 126–27.
57. Ibid., 125–26.
58. Ibid., 117. See also his forthcoming book on John Leighton Wilson.
59. Clarke, *Our Southern Zion*, 119–121; Howe, *History*, II, 411–23.
60. Howe, *History*, II, 411.
61. Ibid., 456. For dollar values, see "Six Ways to Compute."
62. Howe, *History*, I, 323–24.
63. Thompson, *Presbyterians*, 362–77; Ahlstrom, *Religious History*, 464–68, 659–61.
64. *Extracts of the Session Minutes*, 28–33.
65. Clarke, *Our Southern Zion*, 165–81; Clarke, "Strange Case," 41–58.
66. Quoted in Clarke, "Strange Case," 44. See also Thompson, *Presbyterians*, II, 510–29.
67. Quoted in Howe, *History*, II, 458–59.
68. *Ecclesiastical Against Civil Power*, 3–4.
69. Court of Appeals in Chancery, Charleston, July 1842. *Hugh Wislon et al. v. Thomas Legare et al.*

70. Quoted and summarized in Howe, *History*, II, 612–16.

71. Clarke, "Strange Case," 54.

72. Jones and Mills, *History*, 51.

73. Edgar, *South Carolina*, 354–67; Wallace, *South Carolina*, 534–40; Jordan and Stringfellow, *Place Called St. John's*, 139–50.

74. Minton and Law, *Connections*, 36–38.

75. Session Minutes, 1856–1911, 1.

76. Minton and Law, *Connections*, 35.

77. Katherine Dow Ligon, "Ligon Recollections," in Minton and Law, *Connections*, 159–60.

78. Session Minutes, January 13, 1867, 30.

79. Ibid., 31–32.

80. Ibid., October 27, 1867, 35.

81. Ibid., October 20, 1867, 33.

82. Abbott, "Freedman's Bureau," 5–7; Jordan and Stringfellow, *Place Called St. John's*, 151–53.

83. Porcher and Fick, *Sea Island Cotton*, 326–27; See also "Forty Acres and a Mule," http://pbs.org/wgbh/amex/reconstruction/40acres/ps_so15.html (accessed January 31, 2010).

84. Jordan and Stringfellow, *Place Called St. John's*, 162.

85. Ibid., 157.

86. Session Minutes, October 9, 1870, 38.

87. W.S. Bean, "The Presbyterian Church in South Carolina, 1850–1900," in Jones and Mills, *History*, 118.

88. Session Minutes, March 1876, 48–52.

89. Clarke, *Our Southern Zion*, 233.

90. *Minutes*, 76.

91. *All-Black Governing Bodies*, Appendix VI, 177.

92. Clarke, *Our Southern Zion*, 167.

93. For a discussion see Oswald, "Alban Classic," 107.

94. Session Minutes, April 8, 1883, 65.

95. Ibid., March 8, 1885, 71.

96. Ibid., March 28, 1886, 76; April 11, 1886, 77.

97. Ibid., March 26, 1888, April 1888.

98. Ibid., June 9, 1895, 159; November 24, 1895, 166–67.

99. Ibid., April 11, 1886, 77.

100. Ibid., July 11, 1886; October 1886, 79.

101. Ibid., November 24, 1889, 102.

102. Ibid., March 23, 1890, 108–09.

103. Gist, *Presbyterian Women*, 228.

104. Ibid., 230.

105. Session Minutes, November 22, 1891, 121.

106. Ibid., April 15, 1895, 154.

107. Ibid., November 14, 1897, 194.

PART III

108. Oswald, "Minister Effectively," vol. 27, no. 2, 1–7; no. 3, 5–7.

109. Coclanis, *Shadow of a Dream*, 155–56.

110. Session Minutes, July 10, 1898, 207.

111. Scott, *Ministerial Directory*, 554.

112. Fick, *James Island Presbyterian*, 40.

113. October 9, 1898.

114. October 29, 1905.

115. March 28, 1912.

116. March 30, 1919.

117. Minutes, JIMS, April 18, 1915; June 12, 1915; October 9, 1915.

118. Oswald, "Minister Effectively," vol. 27, no. 2, 1–7; no. 3, 5–7.

119. Jordan and Stringfellow, *Place Called St. John's*, 201–13.

120. "Diary of Lida Beckett Andell, 1927–1932," in Jordan and Stringfellow, *Place Called St. John's*, 321–89.

121. Haynie, *John's Island*, 70.

122. Session Minutes, Annual Report, March 1924.

123. Ibid., March 20, 1925.

124. Ibid., September 23, 1928. The date in Jordan and Stringfellow (p. 261) is not correct. The source for the anecdote about the forced sale by Augustus Qualls Jr. is not given.

125. Gist, *Presbyterian Women*, 228.

126. Session Minutes, January 9, 1927.

127. Ibid., January 13, 1929.

128. Ibid., February 9, 1936.

129. Mrs. J.E. Andell, loose-leaf notebook, "History 1930."

130. Session Minutes, November 26, 1933.

131. Ibid., May 12, 1935; October 14, 1934.

132. Fick, *James Island Presbyterian*, 43.

133. Witherspoon, *Ministerial Directory*, 670–71.

134. Session Minutes, September 9, 1945.

135. Ibid., March 23 1947; April 1, 1947.

136. Ibid., January 12, 1947; December 7, 1947; December 21, 1947.

137. Ibid., September 10, 1947; October 5, 1947.

138. Ibid., January 4, 1949; March 21, 1949; March 29, 1950.

139. Ibid., "Catalogue of Communicants, 1896," 305; March 4, 1951; and Congregational Meeting, April 26, 1936.

140. Session Minutes, December 24, 1950.

141. Ibid., July 2, 1952; Minutes and histories, Women of the Church, 1951–52.

142. Session Minutes, March 23, 1954

143. Ibid., October 19, 1953.

144. Ibid., July 15, 1953.

145. Ibid., June 6, 1954

146. Ibid., August 24, 1955.

147. Ibid., October 26, 1954; January 6, 1955.

148. Ibid., January 14, 1955.

149. Ibid., November 13, 1955.

150. Ludwig, *Long Haul*, passim.

151. Session Minutes, August 1960.

152. Ibid., September 26, 1960.

153. Ibid., April 27, 1961.

154. Ibid., July 20, 1961.

155. Ibid., July 17, 1966; February 26, 1967.

156. Ibid., July 7, 1968.

157. Ibid., April 9, 1970.

158. Ibid., October 6, 1968; October 11, 1970.

159. Ibid., August 17, 1969

160. Ibid., September 19, 1971.

161. Ibid., December 10, 1971; Minutes of Congregational Meetings, December 31, 1972.

162. Session Minutes, February 8, 18, 28; March 6; April 6, 8, 15; and June 8, 1973.

163. Oswald, "Minister Effectively," vo. 27, no. 2, 1–7; no. 3, 5–7.

164. Minutes and histories, Women of the Church, 1972–73.

165. *Sandlapper*, February 1971, 58; Minutes and histories, Women of the Church, 1973–74.

166. Session Minutes, September 26, 1974; Minutes of the Congregational Meetings, December 8, 1974.

167. Session Minutes, December 11, 1975.

168. Ibid., April 24, 1975.

169. Ibid., September 21, 1982.

170. Ibid., February 8, 1983.

171. Ibid., February 8, 1983.

172. Minutes of the Congregational Meetings, March 19, 1989.

173. Session Minutes, February 13, 1983.

174. Session Minutes, "Inactive Roll," March 1, 1983.

175. http://www.history.pcusa.org/pres_hist/hist_sites_synod.html (accessed January 17, 2010).

176. Session Minutes, March 9, 1983.

177. Ibid., July 24, 1983, shows specifications.

178. Ibid., October 11, 1983.

179. Ibid., September 13, 1983.

180. Ibid., June 14, 19, 22, 1983.

181. Ibid., December 13, 1983; Minutes of the Congregational Meeting, January 15, 1984.

182. Session Minutes, June 22, 1983.

183. Ibid., October 11, 1983.

184. Ibid., October 9, 1984.

185. Ibid., September 13, 1983.

186. Ibid., April 20, 1983.

187. Ibid., January 10, 1988.

188. Ibid., December 9, 1986.

189. Ibid., January 10, 1988.

190. Ibid., August 10, 1982; March 19, 1989.

191. Ibid., May 15, 1990.

192. Ibid., March 9, 1983

193. Ibid., April 20, 1983.

194. Ibid., December 8, 1981.

195. Ibid., October 11, 1983.

196. Ibid.

197. Ibid., April 11, 1982.

198. Ibid., February 8, 1989.

199. Ibid., May 15, 1990; Minutes of the Congregational Meetings, July 29, 1990.

200. Oswald, "Minister Effectively," vol. 27, no. 2, 1–7, no. 3, 5–7. *Congregational Resource Guide.*

201. Zepke, *Coastal South Carolina*, 150.

202. Session Minutes, April 11, 1995.

203. Ibid., February 27, 1994.

204. Ibid., August 13, 1996.

205. Ibid., April 12, 2000.

206. Ibid., October 13, 1998.

207. Ibid., October 12, 1999.

208. Ibid., February 2, 1997.

209. Ibid., September 12, 2000; November 14, 2000.

210. Ibid., June 11, 2002

211. Ibid., Annual Report, December 1996; Minutes of the Congregation Meeting, December 1, 1996.

212. Session Minutes, June 13, 1995.

213. Ibid., June 9, 1998; August 11, 1998.

214. Ibid., November 14, 2000.

215. Ibid., October 12, 1999; December 14, 1999; January 11, 2000; February 8, 2000; March 14, 2000; April 12, 2000; November 13, 2001.

216. Ibid., November 12, 2002.

217. Ibid., April 26, 1992.

218. Ibid., April 24, 1994.

219. Ibid., March 24, 1995.

220. Ibid., May 9, 1995.

221. Ibid., September 9, 1997.

222. Ibid., October 14, 1997.

223. Ibid., September 21, 1999; September 10, 2001

224. Ibid., Attachment A, May 9, 2000.

225. Ibid., May 11, 1999; February 12, 2002.

226. Ibid., September 14, 1993.

227. Ibid., December 14, 1993.

228. Ibid., March 11, 1997.

229. Ibid., February 13, 2001.

230. Ibid., February 11, 1997.

231. Ibid., August 12, 1997.

232. Ibid., October 9, 1997.

233. Ibid., September 12, 2000; November 14, 2000.

234. Ibid., March 11, 1997; April 8, 1997.

235. Ibid., March 10, 1998.

236. Ibid., August 12, 1997; September 9, 1997; October 14, 1997; November 11, 1997.

237. Ibid., February 10, 1998.

238. Ibid., April 14, 1998; May 12, 1998.

239. Ibid., September 17, 2000.

240. Ibid., May 9, 2000; November 14, 2000.

241. Ibid., August 13, 2002.

242. Ibid.; Minutes of the Congregational Meeting, December 23, 2002.

243. Session Minutes, November 12, 2002.

BIBLIOGRAPHY

CHURCH MANUSCRIPT RECORDS

Brewster Correspondence. Letters from Ichabod Brewster and Anson Brewster, 1811–13. Copies in congregational archives, Johns Island, SC.

Clarkson Correspondence. Letters from Sam Clarkson to M.W. Hills, 1997, 1998. Originals in congregational archives, Johns Island, SC.

Minutes of Congregational Meetings. Johns Island Presbyterian Church, Johns Island, SC. [Sometimes congregational minutes are within Session Minutes. Usually cited by date of congregational meeting.]

Minutes and histories of the Woman's Auxiliary, Women of the Church and Presbyterian Women. Loose-leaf notebooks. Johns Island Presbyterian Church, Johns Island, SC.

Minutes, JIMS. 1913–1919. Bound notebook. Johns Island Missionary Society, Johns Island, SC.

Session Minutes, 1855–2003. Johns Island Presbyterian Church, Johns Island, SC. [Usually cited by date of meeting, but if clarity of reference required it, page number is included.]

Unpublished and Informally Published Works

Abbott, Martin Linton. "The Freedman's Bureau in South Carolina, 1865–1872." PhD diss., Emory University, 1954.

All-Black Governing Bodies. Developed by the Special Committee to Document the History and Contributions of All-Black Governing Bodies of the Presbyterian Church (U.S.A.). Louisville, KY: Office of the General Assembly, 1996.

Hills, Julia C., and Ruth H. McIver, eds. *Johns Island Presbyterian Church Cemetery*. Privately printed, July 1993, 2002.

Hills, Marshall Whilden (Billy). *Johns Island Presbyterian Church Past and Present*. Privately printed, 1996.

Books and Articles

Ahlstrom, Sydney E. *A Religious History of the American People*. New Haven, CT: Yale University Press, 1972.

American and Presbyterian and Reformed Historical Sites, www.history.pcusa.org.

Betts, Albert Deems. *History of South Carolina Methodism*. Columbia, SC: Advocate Press, 1952.

Cameron, Nigel M. de S., ed. *Dictionary of Scottish Church History and Theology*. See esp. "Darien Colony." Edinburgh: T&T Clark, 1993.

Carroll, R.B., comp. *Historical Collections of South Carolina*. New York: Harper and Brothers, 1836.

Clarke, Erskine. *Dwelling Place: A Plantation Epic*. New Haven, CT: Yale University Press, 2005.

———. *Our Southern Zion: A History of Calvinism in the South Carolina Low Country, 1690–1990*. Tuscaloosa: University of Alabama Press, 1996.

———. "The Strange Case of Charleston Union Presbytery: A Pro-Slavery 'New School' Party." *Affirmation* (Fall 1993): 41–58.

———. *Wreslin' Jacob: A Portrait of Religion in the Old South*. Atlanta, GA: John Knox Press, 1979.

Coclanis, Peter A. *The Shadow of a Dream: Economic Life and Death in the South Carolina Low Country, 1670–1920*. New York: Oxford University Press, 1989.

Congregational Resource Guide: Resources for Congregations. Washington, D.C.: Alban Institute, n.d. Available online at www.congregationalresources.org/article0132.asp.

The Ecclesiastical Against the Civil Power! Or The General Assembly of the Presbyterian Church vs. The State of South Carolina, being a Review of the Decree, of the Equity Court of Appeals in the Case of H. Wilson, and Others, vs. The Presbyterian Church of John's Island. By one of the majority. Charleston, SC: Printed by Miller and Browne, 1846.

Edgar, Walter. *South Carolina: A History*. Columbia: University of South Carolina Press, 1998.

Extracts of the Session Minutes of the General Assembly of the Presbyterian Church in the United States of America. Philadelphia, 1818.

Fick, Sarah. *James Island Presbyterian Church: Three Hundred Years of History, 1706–2006*. Charleston, SC: James Island Presbyterian Church Tercentennial Commission, 2006.

Fludd, Eliza C.K. *Biographical Sketches of the Huguenot Solomon Legaré, and of His Family, Extending Down to the Fourth Generation of His Descendents. Also Reminiscences of the Revolutionary Struggle with Great Britain*. Charleston, SC: Edward Perry and Company, 1886.

Gist, Margaret Adams, ed. *Presbyterian Women of South Carolina*. Published by Woman's Auxiliary of the Synod of South Carolina, 1929.

Haynie, Connie Walpole. *Images of America: John's Island*. Charleston, SC: Arcadia Publishing, 2007.

Hewatt, Alexander. *An Historical Account of the Rise and Progress of the Colonies of South Carolina and Georgia*. 2 vols. London: Printed for Alexander Donaldson, 1779.

Hills, Isabel Lofton. "Johns Island Presbyterian Church." *Sandlapper*, February 1971.

Howe, George. *History of the Presbyterian Church in South Carolina*. 2 vols. Columbia, SC: Duffie and Chapman, 1870–73.

Jones, Charles C. *A Catechism, of Scripture, Doctrine and Practice, for Families and Sabbath Schools, Designed also for the Oral Instruction of Colored Persons*. 3rd ed. New York: Leavitt, Trow, 1845.

Jones, F.D., and W. H. Mills, eds. *A History of the Presbyterian Church in South Carolina Since 1850.* Published by the Synod of South Carolina. Columbia, SC: R.L. Bryan Company, 1926.

Jordan, Laylon Wayne, and Elizabeth Stringfellow. *A Place Called St. John's: The Story of John's, Edisto, Wadmalaw, Kiawah, and Seabrook Islands of South Carolina.* Spartanburg, SC: The Reprint Company Publishers, 1998.

Ludwig, Glen. *In It for the Long Haul: Building Effective Long-Term Pastorates.* Herndon, VA: Alban Institute, 2002.

Minton, Lorraine and Donald M. Law. *Connections: The Story of the First Presbyterian Church of Aiken, South Carolina.* Columbia, SC: R.L. Bryan Company, 1984.

Minutes of the General Assembly of the Presbyterian Church in the United States of America. Philadelphia: Presbyterian Board of Publication, 1866.

Oswald, Roy M. "Alban Classic." *Action Information* 17, no. 2 (March/April 1991). Available online at www.alban.org.

———. "How to Minister Effectively in Family, Pastoral, Program, and Corporate Sized Churches." *Action Information* 17, no. 2 (March/April 1991); no.3 (May/June 1991). Available online at www.congregational resources.org/article0132.asp.

Porcher, Richard Dwight, and Sarah Fick. *The Story of Sea Island Cotton.* Charleston, SC: Wyrick and Company, 2005.

Ramsay, David. *Ramsay's History of South Carolina: From Its First Settlement in 1670 to the Year 1808.* Newberry, SC: W.J. Duffie, 1858.

Ruchames, Lewis, ed. *A House Divided Against Itself. The Letters of William Lloyd Garrison.* Vol. 2. Cambridge, MA: Harvard University Press, 1971.

Scott, E.C., ed. *Ministerial Directory of the Presbyterian Church, U.S., 1861–1941.* Austin, TX: Von Boekmann-Jones, Co., 1942.

———. *Ministerial Directory of the Presbyterian Church, U.S., 1861–1941, Revised and Supplemented, 1942–1950.* Atlanta, GA: Hubbard Printing Company, 1950.

Smith, Mark M., ed. *Stono: Documenting and Interpreting a Southern Slave Revolt.* Columbia: University of South Carolina Press, 2005.

Swinton Family Society. "Charts, Legaré: Chart 1." www.swintonfamilysociety.org.

Thompson, Ernest Trice. *Presbyterians in the South.* 3 vols. Richmond, VA: John Knox Press, 1963–73.

Wallace, David Duncan. *South Carolina: A Short History, 1520–1948.* Columbia: University of South Carolina Press, 1961.

Witherspoon, E.D., Jr. *Ministerial Directory of the Presbyterian Church, U.S., 1861–1975.* Atlanta, GA: Darby Printing Company, n.d.

Yon, Katie. *Sea Island Habitat for Humanity: A Mission, A Ministry, A Miracle.* North Charleston, SC: J.R. Rowell Printing Company, 2003.

Zepke, Terrance. *Coastal South Carolina: Welcome to the Lowcountry.* Sarasota, FL: Pineapple Press, 2006.

About the Author

D r. Charles E. Raynal is professor emeritus at Columbia Theological Seminary in Decatur, Georgia.

Visit us at

www.historypress.net